The Samaritan Book of Joshua

Other Books by Charles Siegel:

The History Behind the Bible: The Facts Hidden Behind the Text

The Bible Untangled: Read the Texts that Were Edited Together Thousands of Years Ago to Form the Early Books of the Bible

The P Text Untangled: Making Sense of the Most Puzzling Text of the Bible

Jeremiah Untangled: The Book of Jeremiah Arranged Chronologically with Historical Background

The Original Book of Ecclesiastes

Philosophy of the Earlier Stoics

Philosophy of the Skeptical Academy

Philosophy of the Syncretic Academy

Aeschylus' Prometheus Trilogy

The Good Life: What We Still Know After the Modern Age

A Skeptic's Faith

The Samaritan Book of Joshua

First English Translation of an Ancient Hebrew Text that Challenges the Bible's View of History

Translated with an introduction
by
Charles Siegel

Omo Press

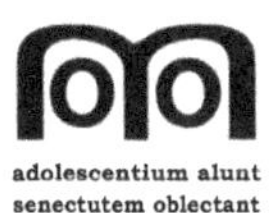

Cover illustration: Meister der Rolle des Josua, Joshua and the two spies, detail from the Joshua Roll, probably 10th Century Byzantine

ISBN: 978-1-941667-60-6

Contents

About the Text

The Hebrew text of the Samaritan Book of Joshua became known to Europeans in 1908, when Moses Gaster produced a text based on three Samaritan manuscripts, correcting many obvious corruptions and errors, and published the Hebrew text with a German translation and commentary first in a periodical (volume LXII of the *Zeitschrit der Deutschen Morgenlandischen Gesellsehaft*, 1908) and then as a book *Das Buch Josua in Hebräish-Samaritaner Rezension: Entdeckt Und Zum Ersten Male Herausgegeben* (1908). It covers the same time period as the Biblical Book of Joshua with just a bit of additional history after Joshua's death.

This Hebrew text is translated into English for the first time here.

Related Books

The Arabic text of the Samaritan Book of Joshua was obviously written much later than the Hebrew text and is very different from the Biblical Book of Joshua, In addition to the period of time covered in the Hebrew text, this Arabic text adds an earlier section about an incident that occurred in the desert when Moses was still alive, and a long later section that extends as far as the Roman period.

It became known to Europeans in the sixteenth century. In 1584, the famous Renaissance scholar and religious leader, Joseph Justus Scaliger, obtained a copy from the Egyptian Samaritans. In 1848, T.W. Juynboll published the Arabic text with a Latin translation as *Chronicon Samaritanum, Arabice Conscriptum, Cui Titulus Est Liber Josuae*. In 1890, Oliver Turnbull Crane published an English translation as *The Samaritan Chronicle or The Book of Joshua Son of Nun*.

Crane's translation is readily available in print and on line. Search for:

The Samaritan Chronicle or the Book of Joshua the Son of Nun, Translated from the Arabic with Notes by Oliver Turnbull Crane (John B. Alden, Publisher, 1890).

The Samaritan version of the Torah is available in an English translation that is laid out in parallel with the Masoretic text traditionally used by Jews:

Benyamim Tsedaka and Sharon Sullivan, *The Israelite Samaritan Version of the Torah: First English Translation Compared with the Masoretic Version* (Eerdmans, 2013).

About this Book

This book uses the following abbreviations:

Jos: Biblical Book of Joshua.

SJos: Hebrew text of the Samaritan Book of Joshua.

SJosA: Arabic text of the Samaritan Book of Joshua.

Quotations from the Bible in this book use the Jewish Publication Society translation of 1917.

Introduction

The Samaritans

The Samaritans have always believed that they are descended from the early Israelites, but the Judeans and later the Jews believed they were alien people whom the Assyrians brought in when they exiled the Israelites.

King David (reigned c. 1010-970 BCE) and King Solomon (reigned c. 970-931 BCE) ruled over a single kingdom that unified the twelve tribes of Israel, but after Solomon's death, the unified kingdom split in two: the ten northern tribes formed the kingdom of Israel, with its capital at Samaria, and the two southern tribes formed the kingdom of Judah, with its capital at Jerusalem. In 722 BCE, the northern kingdom was conquered by Assyria and its people were exiled. At that time, the Assyrians devastated Judah but did not conquer it completely, so it survived until it was conquered and its people were exiled by the Babylonians in 587 or 586 BCE.

The Samaritans believed they were a remnant of the northern kingdom who had not been exiled. They called themselves Israelites rather than Samaritans. They practiced a religion very similar to the religion of ancient Judah with one major exception: their worship centered on Mt. Gerizim and the city of Shechem, which is in a pass between Mt. Gerizim and Mt. Ebal, while the religion of

Judah centered on Jerusalem, about thirty miles to the south.

The Samaritans have their own version of the Torah, which is very similar to the Torah that the Jews use except for two major differences: it is written in archaic Hebrew characters like the characters that all Israelites used before they shifted to the current Hebrew alphabet during the Babylonian exile, and it makes Mt. Gerizim the center of the religion rather than Jerusalem. For example, it says that Abraham went to sacrifice his son Isaac on Mt. Gerizim, while the Jewish Torah says it was on Mt. Moriah, where the Temple in Jerusalem was later built. There are many other relatively minor textual differences, but these are the two most significant differences.[1]

The ancient Judeans denied that the Samaritans were really Israelites and claimed they were people whom the Assyrians brought from other countries to take the place of the exiled Israelites, and that they began to practice a religion like the Judean religion in order to get protection from the local God of the land, as the Bible says:

> [2Kings17:24]And the king of Assyria brought men from
> Babylon, and from Cuthah, and from Avva, and
> from Hamath and Sepharvaim, and placed them in
> the cities of Samaria instead of the children of Isra-
> el; and they possessed Samaria, and dwelt in the cit-
> ies thereof. [25]And so it was, at the beginning of their
> dwelling there, that they feared not the Lord; there-
> fore the Lord sent lions among them, which killed
> some of them. [26]Wherefore they spoke to the king
> of Assyria, saying: 'The nations which thou hast
> carried away, and placed in the cities of Samaria,
> know not the manner of the God of the land; there-

> fore He hath sent lions among them ....' 27Then the king of Assyria commanded, saying: 'Carry thither one of the priests whom ye brought from thence; and let them go and dwell there, and let him teach them the manner of the God of the land.' 28So one of the priests whom they had carried away from Samaria came and dwelt in Bethel, and taught them how they should fear the Lord.

The Judeans called them Samaritans rather than Israelites, after Samaria, the capital city of the northern kingdom, and considered them inferior alien people, whose ideas about religion were worthless.

It was never plausible that the Samaritans would protect themselves by adopting the religion of the land but would make Mt. Gerizim their religious center, though Jerusalem was the main religious center at the time. If they had been misled by a priest from the northern kingdom of Israel, as the Bible claims, he presumably would have taught them that religion should center at Bethel and Dan, where the northern kingdom Israel built temples when it broke with Judah, not at Mt. Gerizim. The Bible says that the Israelite priest came and dwelt at Bethel, where the most important Israelite sanctuary had been, so how did Mt. Gerizim and the adjoining city of Shechem become the center of the Samaritan religion?

Today, we have conclusive evidence that the Samaritans are descended from Israelites. Genetic testing has shown that the remaining Samaritans are descended from the Israelites and closely related to the kohanim[2] – that is, to the descendants of the Levite priests who were in charge of the Temple in Jerusalem. The Bible says that they were taught by a priest from the northern kingdom of Israel, but genetic testing shows us that they are descended from priests from Jerusalem.

Why did the Samaritans chose Mt. Gerizim and Shechem as their religious center? Why does their Torah use archaic Hebrew letters? Why are many of them descended from priests of the Temple in Jerusalem, and why did those priests leave Jerusalem and move to Mt. Gerizim and Shechem? There are some clues to these puzzles.

Shechem, Ebal and Gerizim

The town of Shechem was in a pass between Mt. Ebal to its north and Mt. Gerizim to its south. The town and one of the mountains (Jews said Mt. Ebal and Samaritans said Mt. Gerizim), were the earliest Israelite religious center, but they lost this distinction sometime during the period of the judges.

Both the Biblical and the Samaritan books of Joshua say that Joshua performed two ceremonies at Shechem when the Israelites arrived in Canaan, before the period of the judges began. The Bible says that, after his early victories, Joshua built an altar of unhewn stones on Mt. Ebal and wrote a copy of the law on the stones (Jos 8:30-32), and the Samaritan Book of Joshua says that he built the altar of unhewn stones on Mt. Gerizim and the high priest Eliezer wrote a copy of the law on the stones (SJos 9:14-17). Both books say that, just before his death, Joshua made a covenant with the people at Shechem and set up a stone under an oak there (Jos 24:25-27, SJos 22:16-18), and the Samaritan book adds that the oak was at the foot of Mt. Gerizim.

The Bible makes it clear that Israel's main religious center had already moved to Shiloh by the time of Samuel, as the period of Judges was ending (1Sam 1-4), but it does not say when it moved.

The Samaritans say that the Ark of the Covenant was moved to Shiloh by Eli, the high priest at the time of Samuel, and they believe that, while the Ark was at Mt. Gerizim, there had been a period of peace and prosperity under twelve kings, beginning with Joshua and ending with Samson, followed by a period of decline after the Ark was moved away from Mt. Gerizim (SJosA 40-43). But the claim that Israel was a powerful unified kingdom at this time is clearly a later legend, since archeologists have found that the Israelites had a primitive subsistence economy during this early period.

The Bible's Book of Judges gives us a clue to when the ark might have actually moved. It tells us that Abimelech, son of the powerful judge Gideon by his concubine, lived in Shechem and tried to make himself king by having his relatives in Shechem kill Gideon's other sons. To help him, "...they gave him threescore and ten pieces of silver out of the house of Baal-berith, wherewith Abimelech hired vain and light fellows, who followed him" (Jud 9:4). After he ruled Shechem for three years, some people rebelled against him, and after he defeated them, the rebels "entered into the hold of the house of El-berith" (Jud 9:46), and Abimelech and his army gathered fire wood and burned the building, killing a thousand people.

There are many interpretations of this story, including the claim that Baal-berith and El-berith are two different names for the same sanctuary, which identified Baal with El (that is, with God). But its plainest meaning is that there was a conflict between two rival sanctuaries,

Baal-berith where they worshipped Baal and El-Berith where they worshipped God, and that Baal-berith helped Abimelech so he destroyed El-berith. "Berith" means "covenant," and it seems likely that both these sanctuaries claimed to originate with the covenant that Joshua made with the Israelites in Shechem, one saying it was a covenant to worship Baal and the other saying it was a covenant to worship God.

The Ark might have moved to Shiloh because Abimelech and the Baal worshipers of Shechem threatened and destroyed the religious center of El-Berith. Or this story might be an origin myth based on the fact that there was a conflict between the worship of God and of Baal in Shechem, and the priests moved the Ark to Shiloh to escape it.

At any rate, regardless of when the Ark and the religious center actually moved, it is safe to conclude that the area around Shechem, Mt. Ebal, and Mt. Gerizim was the earliest Israelite religious center, that the Ark moved to Shiloh before the time of Samuel, and that King David moved the Ark to Jerusalem after he created a unified Israelite kingdom (2Sam 6).

The Bible also us tells us that, when the unified kingdom broke up into the northern kingdom of Israel and the kingdom of Judah, King Jeroboam of Israel established two new temples at Dan and Bethel as rivals to Judah's Temple in Jerusalem (1Kings 12:26-30), with a statue of a golden calf in front of each, and did not reestablish the earlier religious centers at Shiloh or at Mt. Ebal, Mt. Gerizim and Shechem.

Why did the Samaritans abandon Jeroboam's temples and reestablish the religious center at Mt. Gerizim and Shechem?

The Origin of the Samaritans

James Montgomery, who wrote the first major book about the Samaritans, theorized that King Josiah of Judah (reigned c. 640-609 BCE) might have contributed to the development of Samaritanism. Josiah carried out a religious reform that ended the worship of pagan gods in Judah, and he also conquered parts of Samaria and extended his reform there, destroying the altar at Bethel (2Kings 23:15). Montgomery says, "Juda's [sic] dominance in Samaria lasted for less than two decades, but we are justified in assuming for this period some rapprochement between the faithful of Joseph and of Juda ...."[3]

But the key idea of Josiah's religious reform was to centralize worship in the temple in Jerusalem, and it is not plausible that he or his followers would have encouraged Samaritan worship at Mt. Gerizim. It is much more plausible that Samaritanism began after Josiah's death.

Josiah and his supporters interpreted all of Israelite history as a lesson showing that kings who worshipped only God would be rewarded with military victory and with prosperity. During Josiah's reign, a new book of the law that made this point was discovered in the Temple in Jerusalem, which scholars believe was an early version of Deuteronomy and which inspired Josiah to begin his religious reform, eliminating pagan worship and centralizing worship in the Temple in Jerusalem (2Kings 22-23).

At first, it seemed that the reform was working. Josiah was victorious in war, conquered parts of what had been the northern kingdom of Israel, and he seemed to be on his way to reconquering all of Israel's lost territory. Even the prophet Jeremiah, who later became famous for prophesying doom and destruction, believed during

Josiah's reign that the ten lost tribes might return to their reconquered territory (Jer 3:6-4:1). But Josiah was killed when he went out to battle Egyptians who were passing through his territory on their way to help the Assyrians fight against the rising Babylonian empire (2Kings 23:29).

It is hard for us to imagine how Josiah's death must have challenged the faith of those to whom he had given so much hope. The Bible explains his death away by saying that, despite his virtue and piety, Josiah and Judah were punished for the sins of Josiah's grandfather, the idolatrous King Manasseh (2Kings 23:26), who introduced worship of pagan gods into the Temple in Jerusalem. But after Josiah's death, the kings who were his successors dropped his reforms, so they obviously did not believe that following Josiah's rules would bring them victory. Josiah's reforms had not brought him the expected military success, so many must have questioned the value of his reforms.

It is plausible that a group of priests from the Temple in Jerusalem decided that Josiah's reforms failed to bring victory because Josiah had chosen the wrong place to worship. Centralizing worship in Jerusalem had not worked for Josiah, and maybe that meant they needed to go back to the earliest Israelite place of worship at Shechem and Mt. Gerizim. The Assyrians had exiled all of the prominent people of the northern kingdom, including its rulers and its priests, leaving behind only poor and uneducated peasants, who identified as Israelites but were not able to manage worship on their own and who would have welcomed these Jerusalem priests as their new religious leaders. Presumably, more Jerusalem priests fled to Shechem after the Babylonians destroyed the Temple in Jerusalem and exiled Judah, and we will see that at least one came after Judah returned from exile.

This movement of priests from Jerusalem to Mt. Gerizim would explain why genetic testing shows that today's Samaritans are related to the kohanim, who are descended from the Jerusalem priests. If most of these priests came before the Babylonian exile, we can see why they continued to use their accustomed archaic Hebrew alphabet after the exiles returned, rather than using the current Hebrew alphabet, which the Judeans adopted during the Babylonian exile, so they wrote the Samaritan Torah in letters similar to archaic Hebrew characters. (We will see more evidence below that Jerusalem priests wrote the Samaritan Book of Joshua.)

The Schism Between Jews and Samaritans

At first, it must have seemed that priests who went to Mt. Gerizim were creating a variant of the Israelite religion. Under the final kings of Judah, worship in Jerusalem was corrupt: the Bible tells us that Josiah's successors all "did that which was evil in the sight of the Lord" (2Kings 23:32,37, 24:9,19), which means they did not uphold monotheism. At the time, the priests who moved to Mt. Gerizim must have seen themselves as practicing proper monotheistic worship at a time when the Temple in Jerusalem had abandoned it.

Then the Babylonians conquered Judah, destroyed the Temple in Jerusalem, and exiled the Judeans, but the Samaritans and their priests remained in place.

It seems likely that schism with the Samaritans began after Jews returned from the Babylonian exile and began rebuilding the Temple in Jerusalem, which they wanted to reestablish as the only legitimate site of worship. The book of Ezra tells us that the "people of the land" wanted to help rebuild the Temple and, after the Jews refused their help, they interfered with the rebuilding of the temple (Ezra 4). It seems likely that this refers to Israelites who remained in Samaria, the obvious candidates who would want to reestablish the Israelite religion, but the Bible does not say they were Israelites because it claims that all Samaritans were foreigners moved in by the Assyrians.

The second Temple was completed in 516 BCE. Not long afterwards, a Samaritan Temple at Mt. Gerizim was built by Sanballat the Horonite, who was the governor of Persian province of Samaria at roughly the same time that Nehemiah was rebuilding the walls of Jerusalem as governor of the Persian province of Yehud or Judah (c. 444-432 BCE, though Nehemiah's dates are disputed). According to Josephus, Sanballat built the Temple for his son-in-law Manasseh, a Jerusalem priest who had been forced out of the Jerusalem Temple because he married Sanballat's daughter.[4] Josephus tells us that the Samaritan Temple resembled the second Temple in Jerusalem;[5] he says it was built in the time of Alexander the Great, but it is generally believed that he is confusing two people named Sanballat and that it was actually built earlier.[6] Archeologists have found that it was built during the Fifth Century BCE.[7]

At about this time, Ezra the Scribe was trying to purify the people by forcing Jewish men to divorce their non-Jewish wives (Ezra 10:10-11), which must have deepened the divide between the Jews and the Samaritans. Yet there was still a flow of people and ideas between the

Jews and the Samaritans. We can see both the division and the continued contact in the story of Sanballat's son-in-law, shunned by the Jews because he married a non-Jew and presiding over the Samaritan Temple, which was influenced by the Torah that the Jews compiled at about the same time.

Nehemiah had Ezra read the Torah to the assembled Jews in Jerusalem, and many Biblical scholars who are not religiously orthodox believe the Torah was edited into its final form at about this time. The Samaritan Torah is so similar to the Jewish Torah that they both must be based on the version created around the time of Ezra. At the time, the Samaritans were still close enough to the Jews to get a copy of the Torah, to believe that Moses gave it to them as well as to the Jews, and to transcribe it from the modern Hebrew alphabet that the Judeans had adopted during the exile in Babylon to their archaic Hebrew alphabet.

The Samaritans changed the Torah to suit their doctrine that Mt. Gerizim was the chosen place, not Jerusalem, and Jews may also have made changes that reflect the schism with Samaritans. The Masoretic text, the standard Jewish text of the Torah, says that God commanded the Israelites to build an altar on Mt. Ebal (Deut 27:4-8), the Samaritan text says the commandment was to build the altar on Mt. Gerizim; but a Dead Sea Scroll with a fragment of Deuteronomy also says the commandment was to build the altar in Mt. Gerizim, leading some scholars to believe that Mt. Gerizim was in the original text and was changed to Mt. Ebal in the Masoretic text.[8]

In about 110 BCE, the Hasmonean King and High Priest, John Hyrcanus, destroyed the Samaritan Temple, devastated Shechem, and slaughtered the Samaritans there as part of a larger military campaign to expand his territory.[9] The Hasmoneans ruled Israel after Judah Macabbee rebelled against the Greeks and purified the Temple in Jerusalem, and they also destroyed the rival Temple on Mt. Gerizim. The split between the Jews and the Samaritans had gone far enough to become murderous.

In 70 CE, the Romans destroyed the Second Temple in Jerusalem. In 132-135 CE, Bar Kokhba led a failed revolt against the Romans; though a small number of Jews remained in Galilee, Israel was largely depopulated, as the Romans killed, enslaved, and expelled the Jews and renamed the province *Syria Palaestina* instead of Judea. For almost two millennia, Jews in exile prayed to return to the land.

The Samaritans were not considered Jews and were not exiled, but they seem to have been even more oppressed staying in place than the Jews were in exile. In 1808, a visitor wrote that there were only thirty families of Samaritans, about 200 people in all, who were found only in Nablus and Jaffa.[10] Their numbers have recovered a bit since then About 380 live on the West Bank in Kiryat Luza, on Mt. Gerizim near the city that was once called Shechem, which the Greeks or Romans rebuilt and renamed Neapolis, and which is now called Nablus, and they speak Arabic as their native language. About 460 live in Holon, near Tel Aviv (which has incorporated Jaffa), and they speak Hebrew as their native language. A scattering live elsewhere in Israel and the West Bank.[11]

Every year at Passover, the Samaritans still sacrifice a lamb on Mt. Gerizim, performing the primitive religious ritual that the earliest Israelites began to practice thousands of years ago to commemorate the exodus from Egypt and that the Samaritans and their ancestors have been performing ever since.

Two Books and Their Source Text

The Biblical and Samaritan books of Joshua seem to be based on an earlier source text written in the northern kingdom of Israel before the Assyrian exile of 722 BCE. We can make out enough of this source text to cast some light on what the northern kingdom believed during the period of the dual kingdoms.

Comparing the Two Books of Joshua

Much of the Hebrew text of the Samaritan Book of Joshua is identical or very similar to the Biblical Book of Joshua, though there are also significant differences.

In some cases, the reasons for the differences are clear. For example, the Samaritan book includes the dates of a some events, which are not in the Biblical book. In fact, it inserts a date right at the beginning of its first chapter:

> [SJos1:1]This is the book of days in which is found the chronicle from the time when Joshua son of Nun arrived in the land of Canaan to this day: In the year two thousand seven hundred four and ninety years after the creation of the world, in the twelfth month after the month of the death of the master of prophets, Moses son of Amram, the peace of the Lord be upon him:

And then it goes on, beginning in verse 1:2, to say the same things that the Biblical book says beginning in verse

1:1. This dating is more evidence that the Samaritan book was written by a group of priests who originated in the Temple of Jerusalem and came to Samaria, as the genetic evidence that the Samaritans are descended from kohanim suggests. The P text of the Torah, which was written by Jerusalem priests, includes a timeline that lets them calculate the years of important events.[12] The group of priests who moved from Jerusalem to Mt. Gerizim kept this focus on chronology.

Because it was written by Jerusalem priests, who believed they were descended from Aaron, the Samaritan Book of Joshua gives a more prominent place to the high priest Eliezer son of Aaron than the Biblical Book of Joshua does. For example, in the Biblical book, the spies report to Joshua (Jos 2:24), but in the Samaritan book, they report to Joshua, Eliezer, and the heads of the tribes (SJos 2:26). In the Biblical book, the Hivites make a covenant with Joshua (Jos 9:6 et seq), but in the Samaritan book they make a covenant with Joshua and Eliezer (SJos 10:3 et seq). In the Biblical book, Joshua builds an altar and writes the law on it (Jos 8:32), but in the Samaritan book, Joshua builds the altar and Eliezer writes the law on it (SJos 9:17). Likewise, the P text of the Torah has Moses and Aaron do many things together that the other texts have Moses do alone,[13] because the authors were Jerusalem priests who wanted to make their ancestor Aaron more important, as the authors of the Samaritan Book of Joshua wanted to make Eliezer son of Aaron more important.

It is also clear why the Samaritan book includes a lengthy history of Joshua's war with Shobach and coalition of surrounding nations after the conquest of Canaan was complete (SJos 16-21), but the Biblical text does not. The Samaritans considered Joshua the greatest military hero of Israelite history, but the Judeans considered King David the greatest military hero, and the Bible has King David defeat Shobach (2Sam 10:15-19), so the editors of the Bible had to pull the defeat of Shobach out of their book of Joshua.

Of course, it is also clear why the Samaritan book continues the story beyond Joshua's death to the time when the Torah was written down in Shechem, supposedly just as Moses had spoken it (SJos 23-24), and that this is the same Torah used in Shechem "to this day" (SJos 24:2). They wanted to legitimize the Samaritan version of the Torah and to emphasize the central position of Mt. Gerizim in the Israelite religion. It is even more obvious why the Samaritan book says Joshua built a temple on Mt. Gerizim (SJos 13:1-10), while the Biblical book does not.

Though it is not as obvious, we can see at least part of the reason why the Biblical and Samaritan books of Joshua have very different accounts of the territories of the nine and a half tribes who crossed the Jordan (Jos 13:7-19:51, SJos 14), though they both have the same account of the territories of the two and a half tribes that did not cross the Jordan (Jos 13:8-13:33, SJos 13:11-37). The Samaritan book has just one chapter for the division of territory among these tribes (SJos 14), while the Biblical book has two chapters for Judah alone, including one for the Calebites (Jos 14-15). The borders of Judah in the Biblical book are identical to the borders of Judah in Josiah's time, and it includes a very long list of cities in the territory that are identical to the cities that existed in Josiah's time, including some cities that had not existed earlier.[14] The Biblical book also has four chapters about allocation of territory to the other tribes (Jos 16-19), with much more details about their boundaries than the Samaritan book. Clearly, the Biblical book changed the source text to reflect conditions in Judah during the reign of Josiah, when this book was being rewritten and incorporated into the Bible around the time of Josiah: we have seen that Judeans were optimistic at this time that Josiah would reconquer the Biblical territory of the tribes and the northern tribes would return from exile (Jer 3:6-4:1), so they specified the boundaries of their territories precisely to prepare for their return.

The Source Text

There are other differences between the two books, but the common features are more striking than the differences. Both tell the stories of how the Lord commanded Joshua, how Joshua prepared to enter Canaan, how Rahab the harlot helped Joshua's spies in Jericho, how the Israelites crossed the Jordan and destroyed Jericho, how they initially lost at Ai because an Israelite had taken spoil from Jericho, how they destroyed Ai, how they were tricked into making a covenant with the Hivites, how they defeated a coalition formed by the king of Jerusalem (also called Jebus), how they defeated a series of cities from Gaza to Goshen, how they defeated a coalition formed by Jabin king of Hazor, how land was given to the tribes that remained east of the Jordan, and how Joshua made a covenant with the people when he died.

In these stories, the two books use identical or very similar language, sometimes with no alteration, sometimes with a word or phrase changed or omitted, sometimes with longer passages added or omitted – but despite the changes, the same stories are told largely in the same language.

There are two possible ways to explain how two books can tell the same stories in the same language: either one of the books is based on the other, or both books are based on a common source text.

If one were based on the other, it seems the Biblical Book of Joshua would have been written first, and the Samaritan book would have to be based on it.

One piece of evidence that the Biblical book was written first is the description of the stones that Joshua set up to commemorate crossing the Jordan. The Biblical book says:

> Jos 4:9 Joshua also set up twelve stones in the midst of the Jordan, in the place where the feet of the priests that bore the ark of the covenant stood; and they are there unto this day.

But the Samaritan book says:

> SJos 4:7 And Joshua son of Nun raised twelve stones in the midst of the Jordan, in the place of the feet of the priests who carried the ark of the covenant of the Lord, and they were there.

The stones were still there when the Biblical book was written, but they were no longer there when the Samaritan book was written, so it eliminated "unto this day," leaving the awkward conclusion "and they were there."

Our speculations about the origin of the Samaritans also imply that the Biblical book was written earlier, because it was incorporated into the Deuteronomistic history in the time of Josiah, while priests did not go from

Jerusalem to Mt. Gerizim and found Samaritanism until after the death of Josiah.

Yet we can also see cases where the Biblical book is clearly modifying an earlier text, showing that it was not the earliest Book of Joshua. For example, the famous Biblical passage where Joshua stops the sun and the moon is not in the Samaritan book, and the Biblical book mentions the source of this added story:

> Jos 10:13 And the sun stood still, and the moon stayed, until the nation had avenged themselves of their enemies. Is not this written in the book of Jashar?

Another case where the Biblical book clearly adds something to an earlier text comes at the very end of its its description of the inheritance of Judah:

> Jos 15:63 And as for the Jebusites, the inhabitants of Jerusalem, the children of Judah could not drive them out; but the Jebusites dwelt with the children of Judah at Jerusalem, unto this day.

This verse stands out because it is at odds with the entire rest of the Biblical book of Joshua, which says very clearly that Joshua overcame and destroyed all of the Canaanites except the Hivites, who tricked Joshua into making a covenant with them. This verse looks like a later addition because of its location at the very end of the description of the territory of Judah and because it just baldly states that Joshua could not drive out the Jebusites, without any story to explain it like the lengthy story of the Hivites. The editors who compiled the Biblical text were in Jerusalem, so they added this verse to account for the presence of the Jebusites, whom they could not help seeing around them; presumably, the authors of the source text were in the northern Kingdom of Israel, so they were less likely to notice the Jebusites in Jerusalem.

In the Biblical book, the most prominent example of material from the source text that should have been removed but was retained by mistake is at the very beginning:

> [Jos 1:1]...the Lord spoke unto Joshua the son of Nun, Moses' minister, saying: [2]'Moses My servant is dead; now therefore arise, go over this Jordan, thou, and all this people, unto the land which I do give to them, even to the children of Israel. [3]Every place that the sole of your foot shall tread upon, to you have I given it, as I spoke unto Moses. [4]From the wilderness, and this Lebanon, even unto the great river, the river Euphrates, all the land of the Hittites, and unto the Great Sea toward the going down of the sun, shall be your border.

But there is nothing in the Biblical book fulfilling the prophecy that Joshua will conquer the land of the Hittites or extend his empire to the Euphrates. According to the Biblical book, Joshua conquers Canaan and distributes the land to the tribes of Israel, but there are no further conquests that give him a larger empire.

At the beginning of the Samaritan Book of Joshua, there is virtually identical text (SJos 1:2-5), and it is fulfilled in the Samaritan book. That book says that, after conquering Canaan and distributing its land, Joshua was threatened by a coalition of surrounding kings from outside of Canaan led by King Shobach, and he wiped out their armies (SJos 16-21). Conquering this land outside of Canaan would extend Joshua's empire, as prophesied at the beginning of the book.

These conquests beyond Canaan must have been in the source text and been removed by the Judean editors who created the Biblical Book of Joshua, because, in their version of history, King David is the one who conquered a large empire that extended as far as the Euphrates (2Sam 8). In the Bible, it is also David rather than Joshua who defeats Shobach (2Sam 10:15-19).

The Northern Version of Israelite History

We are familiar with the Judean version of Israelite history in the Bible, in the books of Joshua, Samuel, and Kings. This history centers on the the purity of worship at the temple in Jerusalem, and its hero is King David, who made Jerusalem the center of Israelite worship and was rewarded with military victories that let him conquer a vast empire.

Thinking about the source text of the two books of Joshua, we can see that the northern kingdom of Israel had a view of history that made what they called "Mt. Gerizim Bethel" the center of Israelite worship, identifying Jeroboam's temple at Bethel with the site Joshua established on Mt. Gerizim. Its hero was Joshua, who built an altar on Mt. Gerizim, had the Israelites make a covenant to worship only God, and was rewarded with military victories that let him conquer a vast empire.

The Bible tells us that when Jeroboam became the first king of the northern kingdom of Israel, he built two temples, one in Dan at the northern end of his kingdom and one in Bethel at the southern end of his kingdom (1Kings 12:28-29), where it would attract people on their way to Jerusalem to sacrifice. Bethel was the more important of these two new temples, where Jeroboam himself sacrificed (1Kings 12:32).

In the Samaritan Book of Joshua, there are many references to "Mt. Gerizim Bethel," which seem to be left over from the source text. The Samaritan book tells us that Joshua conquered the Canaanite city of Luz "which is in Mt. Gerizim, which is Bethel" (SJos 9:11). Then:

> SJos 9:14 And Joshua son of Nun built an altar of stones on Mt. Gerizim, which is Bethel, as Moses commanded the children of Israel according to the word of the Lord, unhewn stones. 15 And there went up from it burnt offerings and peace offerings. 16 And fire came out from the Lord and consumed what was on the altar.

And there are seventeen subsequent references in the Samaritan Book to "Mt. Gerizim Bethel."

The source book of Joshua apparently wanted to legitimize the northern kingdom's temple at Bethel by identifying it with Joshua's altar at Mt. Gerizim, though Bethel is actually a separate city about fifteen miles south of Shechem, which is in a pass with Mt. Ebal to its north and Mt. Gerizim to its south.

By insisting the Joshua built an altar on Mt. Gerizim, the source text brought Joshua's altar further south and closer to Bethel, making it a bit more plausible to identify the two. By contrast, the Biblical book has Joshua build the altar on Mt. Ebal (Jos 8:30-31), which is to the north of Shechem and further from Bethel, making it harder to identify the two. And, of course, the editors of the Biblical book deleted all references to "Mt. Gerizim Bethel," because they did not want to legitimize the northern kingdom's temple at Bethel by connecting it with Joshua.

Why did the Samaritans keep the phrase "Mt. Gerizim Bethel" in their book of Joshua when they themselves had nothing to do with Jeroboam's temple at Bethel and worshipped on Mt. Gerizim itself? Bethel is Hebrew for "the house of God," and maybe the Samaritans took the word literally and thought the phrase just meant "Mt. Gerizim the house of God." But the source text was written before the Assyrians exiled the ten northern tribes, when they were still worshiping at the temple in Bethel, and at that time, everyone would have immediately recognized that the phrase referred to Bethel, where the temple was.

The heroes of the of the two versions of history both defeated Shobach and conquered an empire that extended to the Euphrates.

They also used a similar phrase when they died. As he was dying David said to Solomon, "I go the way of all the earth" (I Kings 2:2). And as he was dying, Joshua said to the Israelites "I am going the way of all the earth" (Jos 23:14) – according to the Biblical book but oddly not according to the Samaritan book of Joshua.

Finally, the Samaritan book of Joshua repeatedly calls him King Joshua, and it also says:

> SJos 17:2 And the man heard their words and went and came to Joshua son of Nun. 3 And he found him sitting on his royal throne

making Joshua the first king who successfully unified all the tribes, rather than David.

Both Joshua and David were said to be the king who unified Israel, defeated Shobach, extended his empire to the Euphrates, and spoke similar dying words.

If the northern kingdom wrote down more of their narrative of history, it did not survive. We can easily imagine what they thought of King Solomon, based on the narrative in the Bible saying that the unified monarchy split in two because the northern tribes complained about how Solomon oppressed them, and his successor, King Rehoboam, said he would oppress them even more severely (1Kings 12:1-16). They obviously thought he was an oppressor as well as being a heretic for building a temple in Jerusalem.

It is harder to imagine what they thought of David, who tried hard to unify the kingdom and treat all the tribes fairly, but whom they must have considered a heretic because he moved the Ark to Jerusalem and centered worship there rather than in "Mt. Gerizim Bethel."

Even with the small amount of information that we have, it is striking to think that, in Biblical times, there was a northern narrative of Israelite history that was at odds with the Judean narrative in the Bible that we are familiar with.

The plausible explanation for this difference is that the earlier source book was written in the northern kingdom of Israel before the Assyrian conquest and exile, and that the northern kingdom had a different version of Israelite history than the one we are familiar with from the Bible. According to the history books of the Bible, Joshua conquered Canaan, but King David and King Solomon (who were both Judeans) created a powerful, wealthy Israelite empire that the world admired, because they centered worship in Jerusalem (in the territory of Judah). According to the northern Israelite history, Joshua (who was an Ephraimite) created a powerful empire with its worship centered in what they call Mt. Gerizim Bethel (in the territory of Ephraim).

The Books of Joshua in History

The Biblical and Samaritan books of Joshua and their common source text are all blood-thirsty. In fact, they are what we today call genocidal. For example, after Joshua conquers a series of cities, both books say:

> Jos 11:19/SJos 12:19 There was not a city that made peace with the children of Israel, save the Hivites the inhabitants of Gibeon; they took all in battle. 20 For it was of the Lord to harden their hearts, to come against Israel in battle, that they might be utterly destroyed, that they might have no favour, but that they might be destroyed, as the Lord commanded Moses.

This quote is from the Bible, and the translation of the Samaritan book is a bit different, but the original Hebrew is exactly the same in both, which means that this passage comes directly from the source text.

Both books also refer elsewhere to the command to slaughter all the Canaanites (Jos 9:24/SJos 10:24, Jos 11:14-15/SJos 12:14-15). The descriptions of how Joshua wipes out entire peoples are also identical or similar in both books.

The Bible is often criticized for being blood-thirsty, but it is not the only strand of thinking in the Bible. It does not reflect the actual early history of Israel: archeologists have found that there was no slaughter of Canaanites when the Israelites appeared. The blood-thirstiness arose in response to later events. We know how it originated in Judah, and we can also begin to see how it originated in the northern kingdom of Israel.

The Deuteronomistic Reform

The Bible has enough of the history of Judah that we can see how this attitude originated there. After the Assyrians destroyed and exiled the northern kingdom of Israel in 722 BCE, the Judeans lived in fear that the same would happen to them, and this fear led them to swing between religious extremes.

King Hezekiah of Judah (reigned c. 716-687 BCE) lived at the time when the Assyrians invaded, devastated, and exiled the northern kingdom, and he hoped to save his kingdom by a strict religious reform that banned all pagan worship and concentrated Judean worship in Jerusalem (2 Kings 18). The Assyrians invaded Judah, destroyed most of its cities, devastated its countryside, and besieged Jerusalem, but during the siege, the Bible tells us, the Assyrian soldiers were killed by an angel (2 Kings 19:35), so Jerusalem survived. This probably means that they were killed by a plague, since an earlier text says killed by an angel when it clearly means killed by a plague (II Sam 24:15-16).

The Bible sees the survival of Jerusalem as a sign of the success of Hezekiah's reform, but the devastation of Judah's other cities and countryside might not have seemed like such a great success to people at the time. Hezekiah's son, King Manasseh (reigned 687–643 BC) must not have been satisfied with the results of his father's reform, since he went to the opposite extreme:

> [2Kings 21:3]he built again the high places which Hezekiah his father had destroyed; and he reared up altars for Baal, and made an Asherah, as did Ahab king of Israel, and worshipped all the host of heaven, and served them. .... [5]And he built altars for all the

> host of heaven in the two courts of the house of the Lord. And he made his son to pass through the fire, and practised soothsaying, and used enchantments, and appointed them that divined by a ghost or a familiar spirit.... [7]And he set the graven image of Asherah, that he had made, in the [Temple].

We can easily imagine that Manasseh believed Hezekiah's reforms had not worked well enough, so he decided to also invoke protection from other powers.

Manansseh's son, King Amon, reigned only two years and died young, so his son, Josiah (reigned c. 641-610 BCE) became king at the age of 8. When Josiah was 25 years old, the Temple was being renovated and the workers there discovered a book of the law that the Bible says recorded the words of Moses but had not been known before, and this book inspired Josiah to begin a strict religious reform (2Kings 22:8-13), banning all pagan worship and concentrating worship in the Temple in Jerusalem. At first, this reform seemed to work and bring military success: Josiah reconquered some Israelite territory that had been lost to the Assyrians, but as we have seen, Josiah was killed in about 609 BCE when he went to battle with Egyptians passing through his territory (2 Kings 23:29), and his reform was abandoned.

Today, Biblical scholars who are not religiously orthodox generally believe that the book found in the Temple was an early version of the book of Deuteronomy, where Moses clearly says that the Israelites should wipe out all of the Canaanites so they are not misled into worshipping their gods, and also says that worshiping only the Lord will bring them security and prosperity, while worshipping pagan gods will lead to their country being devastated and their being exiled -- a warning inspired by the devastation and exile of the northern kingdom of Israel.

Scholars who are not orthodox generally believe that the history books that follow, partly written around the time of Josiah and also incorporating earlier texts, are meant to illustrate the point of Josiah's reform, that worshipping only the Lord in Jerusalem will lead to military victory, so these books are called the Deuteronomistic history.

According to this didactic version of history, King David moved the Ark of the Covenant and the center of worship to Jerusalem, so he conquered a huge empire. King Solomon built the Temple in Jerusalem, so he kept his empire and became fabulously wealthy and wise. But in his old age, Solomon let his foreign wives worship pagan gods in the high places overlooking Jerusalem, so he was punished by his son's losing most of his kingdom when the northern kingdom of Israel broke from Judah.

After that, the two kingdoms were much weaker than they had been at the time of David and Solomon, according to this didactic history, because they did not worship only the Lord in Jerusalem. All the kings of Israel "did what was evil in the sight of the Lord" by worshipping in Dan and Bethel instead of Jerusalem, and most of them also allowed pagan religions. Likewise, most of the kings of Judah "did what was evil in the sight of the Lord" by allowing pagan religion, with Hezekiah and Josiah as conspicuous exceptions.

The early source text of the two books of Joshua obviously was ripe to be incorporated into the Deuteronomistic history, since it says that the Lord commanded Joshua to wipe out all the pagans, that Joshua made covenants with the children of Israel to worship only the Lord, and that as a result, Joshua had great military success. The editors of the Deuteronomistic history removed Joshua's conquest of a large empire, so that Joshua's conquests would not rival King David's. And they replaced Mt. Gerizim with Mt. Ebal and removed references to "Mt. Gerizim Bethel," to avoid legitimizing the northern kingdom's temple at Bethel. But with these changes and a few others, it was an excellent example of the principles of the book of Deuteronomy and of Josiah's reform.

The extreme blood-thirstiness of the Deuteronomistic history was a result of the extreme situation that Judah was in after the reign of Hezekiah. Assyria had devastated, conquered, and exiled the northern kingdom of Israel and devastated and almost conquered Judah. Kings of Judah swung between religious extremes in a desperate attempt to protect themselves – from Hezekiah's monotheistic reform to Manasseh's human sacrifice and pagan worship, to Josiah's monotheistic reform, which included Deuteronomy's call for genocide to avoid being tempted into pagan worship. These extremes were the result of desperation, and we cannot assume that the call for genocide was part of the original Israelite religion, any more than Manasseh's human sacrifice was part of the original Israelite religion.

The Israelite Reform

The source text of the books of Joshua was also genocidal and was probably written as part of a similar but earlier religious reform in the northern kingdom of Israel.

The obvious candidate is the reform that began with the attack on Baal worship by Elijah, Elisha and other prophets during the reigns of King Ahab (c. 874-853 BCE), King Ahaziah (c. 853-852 BCE), and King Jehoram (852-841 BCE), which culminated in a violent religious reform under King Jehu (841-814 BCE), who wiped out Baal worship.

Under the reign of these earlier kings, Israel suffered from droughts and from war with the Arameans. Though it tends to get lost among all the other details in the Bible's history, there is little doubt that this religious reform was meant to protect Israel and improve its fortunes, as Josiah's reform was meant to protect Judah. Let's look at the suffering and violence of the time before the reform.

King Ahab of Israel married the princess Jezebel, a Baal worshiper from from the Phoenician city of Sidonia, and he

> [1Kings 16:32]reared up an altar for Baal in the house of Baal, which he had built in Samaria. [33]And Ahab made the Asherah; and Ahab did yet more to provoke the Lord, the God of Israel, than all the kings of Israel that were before him.

According to the Bible, Elijah cursed Ahab and caused a drought (1Kings 17:1). Jezebel killed all the prophets of the Lord except fifty who were hidden (1Kings 18:3). After three years of drought, at a time of severe famine, Elijah had his famous contest with the priests of Baal: they built an altar and called on their gods without success to accept their sacrifice, and then Elijah built an altar and called on the Lord to accept his sacrifice, a fire immediately came from heaven and consumed his sacrifice, and Elijah told the Israelites who had been watching that they should kill all the prophets of Baal (1Kings 18:40). This sacrifice ended the drought in Israel, but Jezebel threatened to kill Elijah, and he had to flee to the wilderness (1Kings 18:2-3).

Then Ben Haddad, the king of Aram, led a coalition of thirty-two kings and besieged Samaria, the capital city. Ahab agreed to give Ben Haddad all his gold, silver, wives and children in exchange for ending the siege (1Kings 20:3-4), but Ben Haddad insisted on also coming into Samaria to take more, and Ahab managed to break the siege and defeat the Arameans. A year later, the Israelites defeated the Arameans in Aphek (1Kings 20:26-34).

Later, Jezebel got false witnesses to accuse Naboth the Jezreelite of cursing God and the king, so Naboth could be killed and Ahab could steal his vineyard. Elijah came and prophesied that the dogs would lick up Ahab's blood and eat Jezebel's body (1Kings 21). Three years later, Ahab made an alliance with Judah to attack the Arameans, he was killed in battle, and the dogs licked up his blood (1 Kings 22).

About this time, Elijah died – the Bible says, he was carried to heaven in a flaming chariot – and his powers passed to Elisha (2 Kings 2).

Later, Ben Haddad came to besiege Samaria, the capital city of Israel, and the hunger there was so extreme that a mother boiled and ate her own son (2 Kings 6:24-29). But the Lord broke the siege by making the Arameans believe falsely that a huge army was coming to attack them (2 Kings 7:5-8).

Then, there was a famine that lasted for seven years, as Elisha predicted (2 Kings 8:1-3).

Elisha told one of the sons of the prophets to go and anoint Jehu as king to replace Jehoram. As the new king, Jehu ordered his soldiers to throw Jezebel out of the window, and they trampled on her body; when they went to bury her, they found the dogs had eaten her body, as Elijah had predicted (2 Kings 9:36). Jehu also killed Ahab's seventy sons and piled up their heads in two heaps at the gate of Jezreel (2 Kings 10:8). He killed "all that remained of the house of Ahab in Jezreel, and all his great men, and his familiar friends, and his priests, until there was left him none remaining" (2 Kings 10:11). Finally, Jehu called Baal worshippers from all over Israel to Samaria to attend a great sacrifice in the House of Baal; once they were there, he appointed eighty soldiers to kill them all, and he broke down and burned the House of Baal. The author of the text seems to enjoy the dogs licking Ahab's blood and eating Jezebel's body and to enjoy those piles of heads at the gates of Jezreel.

This was a blood-thirsty time and a blood-thirsty religious reform that could easily have produced the blood-thirsty source text of the books of Joshua.

The Bible's story is filled with digressions that make it hard to see that Israel had faced a long period of famine and war before this reform. During the thirty-three years from the beginning of Ahab's reign to the end of Jehoram's reign, there were ten years of famine, and there were repeated wars with Aramea, including a siege of Samaria that created such extreme hunger that a woman ate her baby son.

The religious reformers obviously believed the Lord had caused all this suffering as a punishment for Baal worship and hoped that their reform would bring them prosperity and military victory. They were in a desperate situation, so they were willing to carry out a desperate and vicious reform to save themselves.

The reform does not seem to have worked, since the Bible tells us that, under Jehu, Hazael and the Arameans conquered Israel's territories to the east of the Jordan River, the territories of Reuben, Gad, and half the tribe of Manasseh (2 Kings 10:32-33), and Aramea continued to defeat Israel during the reigns of Jehu's son and grandson, who both continued his reforms (2 Kings 13).

The Bible sums up Jehu's reforms from its usual Judah-and-Jerusalem-centered perspective by saying:

> [2Kings 10:28]Thus Jehu destroyed Baal out of Israel.
> [29]Howbeit from the sins of Jeroboam the son of Nebat, wherewith he made Israel to sin, Jehu departed not from after them, the golden calves that were in Beth-el, and that were in Dan.

The Judeans thought the reform failed because it did not center worship in Jerusalem.

But the northern kingdom of Israel obviously had a different view of this reform. We can get some idea of their religious views from what we can reconstruct of the source text of the Book of Joshua.

Their reform legitimized Bethel as the most important place of worship by identifying it with the altar that Joshua built at "Mt. Gerizim Bethel." It clearly considered Bethel more legitimate than the later religious center that David and Solomon founded in Jerusalem.

It was strictly monotheistic and suppressed the worship of pagan gods, as we can see from the covenant that Joshua makes with the people before his death. After describing all the things that the Lord did for the Israelites, Joshua says in the Biblical book:

> [Jos 24:14]Now therefore fear the Lord, and serve Him in sincerity and in truth; and put away the gods which

> your fathers served beyond the River, and in Egypt; and serve ye the Lord. 15And if it seem evil unto you to serve the Lord, choose you this day whom ye will serve; whether the gods which your fathers served that were beyond the River, or the gods of the Amorites, in whose land ye dwell; but as for me and my house, we will serve the Lord.' 16And the people answered and said: 'Far be it from us that we should forsake the Lord, to serve other gods;

And he says something very similar in the Samaritan book (SJos 22:10), so this passage must come from the source text.

There was also a book of the law that codified the ideas behind this reform, as Deuteronomy codified the ideas behind Josiah's reform. The Biblical book says that, after admonishing the Israelites in this way:

> Jos 24:25So Joshua made a covenant with the people that day, and set them a statute and an ordinance in Shechem. 26And Joshua wrote these words in the book of the law of God; and he took a great stone, and set it up there under the oak that was by the sanctuary of the Lord. 27And Joshua said unto all the people: 'Behold, this stone shall be a witness against us;

And the Samaritan book says something similar but with more on the role of the priests and Mt. Gerizim (SJos 22:16), so the source text must mention this book of the law.

The source text also mentions what seems to be a different text of the law, written on the altar Joshua built. The Biblical book says that, after he built an altar on Mt. Gerizim:

> Jos 8:32 And he [Joshua] wrote there upon the stones a copy of the law of Moses, which he wrote before the children of Israel.

And the Samaritan book says something very similar but with Eliezar son of Aaron the priest writing the law, rather than Joshua, so the source text must also mention this version of the law.

The texts use the word Torah to mean law, but at the time the source text was written, the Torah did not exist in its present form, which is obviously much too long to write on a stone altar. They used the word "Torah" simply to mean the law of Moses, rather than the canonized Torah we have today. But the written Israelite law from the time of Jehu's reform has not survived.

The History Behind the Legends

Archaeologists have found that the actual process of Israelite settlement in Canaan was very different from the legends about Joshua's military conquests. Based on the number of cities and agricultural settlements that existed at various times in prehistory, archeologists have found that the Canaanite hill country lost most of its population because of a drought that began in about 1550 BCE[15] and lasted until about the time when the Israelites appeared shortly before 1200 BCE.[18] The Israelites settled peacefully in the nearly empty hill country and avoided the coastal plain and the valleys, which were already occupied.

We have all heard of Joshua's legendary destruction of Jericho, but in reality, the Egyptians destroyed Jericho in about 1500 BCE,[17] long before the Israelites came, and it was not rebuilt, presumably because of the drought. The story that Joshua destroyed Jericho by blowing trumpets, so the walls came tumbling down, is a myth meant to explain the origin of the very visible ruins of a city that had actually been destroyed much earlier than the time of Joshua.

The legend of how the Hivites survived by tricking Joshua, telling him that they were not really local Canaanites but lived far away (Jos 9, SJos 10) is also an origin myth. Scholars differ about who the Hivites were, but this legend obviously began as a myth explaining why the Jezreel Valley was still full of Canaanites, though Joshua had supposedly been commanded to slaughter all the Canaanites. In reality, the map of early territories of the different tribes makes it clear that Israelites settled in the empty hill country and skipped over the Jezreel Valley, which was more fertile than the hills, so Canaanites had continued to live and farm there when the drought struck the hill country.

The Biblical book also says that Joshua did not drive out the Jebusites from Jerusalem, so "the Jebusites dwelt with the children of Judah at Jerusalem, unto this day" (Jos 15:63). Actually, Jerusalem was one of the few cities in the hill country that continued to be inhabited during the drought, presumably because the prominent rock on the top of Mt. Moriah made it a Canaanite religious center. Initially the Israelites skipped over this area because it was occupied by Canaanites, and centuries later, King David conquered it and made it his capital. The First and Second Temples were built on this rock, and now the Dome of the Rock is there.

The early Israelites did not slaughter the Canaanites to take their land, as the books of Joshua claim. They settled in the empty parts of the hill country, avoiding the few places where Canaanites already lived.

Some passages in the Bible also show us that the early Israelites did not believe they were commanded to slaughter the inhabitants of the land, as the books of Joshua and Deuteronomy claim.

Much of the Bible's story of King David is taken from a document called the court history of David, which was apparently written before the Deuteronomistic reform and incorporated into the Deuteronomistic history because the authors admired King David and wanted to preserve everything known about him, even if it did not always support their ideology. It tells the story of how David fell in love with Bathsheba, how he sent her husband, Uriah the Hittite, to die on the front lines of the war so he could marry her, how Nathan the Prophet condemned what David did, and how David immediately rent his clothing and repented his sin (2 Sam 11:1-12:15). The prophet considered Uriah's life as valuable as anyone else's and his marriage with an Israelite woman as valid as any marriage, though Uriah was a Hittite rather than an Israelite – and King David realized the Prophet was right.

The books of Joshua show a unified Israelite nation conquering Canaan, but the earlier legends in the Book of Judges show that the early Israelite tribes were not unified and lived in relative peace. The compilers of the Deuteronomistic history made their usual point by focusing on judges who were successful militarily, but during the two centuries or so of the period, the book of Judges describes a relatively small number of conflicts with surrounding peoples, most involving only one tribe, implying that most people lived in peace during most of this period. Only after the Philistines settled on the coast was there enough of a military threat that the Israelites had to unify under a king with a standing army to defend themselves.

Archeologists have found that, during the period of the judges, Israelites lived in small villages of one hundred to a few hundred people, with subsistence economies based on farming and herding, with houses that were all about the same size, implying that there was little inequality,[18] and with no fortifications,[19] implying that they lived in a relatively peaceful time when there was little need for self defense.

They have also found that, at the time of David, Israel still had a primitive economy and would not have been able to rule the large empire that David supposedly conquered; there were only about 45,000 people in all of David's unified kingdom.[20] Some scholars used to claim that the stories of David were myths with no historical basis at all, but in 1993, archeologists discovered an inscription mentioning the house of David on an Aramean victory stele,[21] the first mention of David outside of the Bible, confirming that he actually existed. Most likely, the historical David formed a standing army that allowed him to unify the Israelite tribes, to defend them from the Philistines, and to demand tribute from some of the surrounding peoples.[22]

At the time of Solomon, Israel still had a primitive economy, which would not have been able to generate Solomon's legendary wealth. Presumably, he got his reputation for opulence because of his great building projects, the Temple and his palace in Jerusalem. But he built these by oppressing the Israelites with high taxes and possibly with forced labor, and even by giving twenty cities in the northern part of Israel to Hiram of Tyre in exchange for his help in building (1Kings 9:10-14). The Israelites rebelled unsuccessfully against Solomon (1 Kings 11:26-40), and after his death, they rebelled successfully against his son Rehoboam when he said he would continue Solomon's oppressive policies (1Kings 12:1-21). The legends say Solomon was rich, wise and just, but in reality, his extravagance destroyed the unified kingdom.

We all know and love the legends about Joshua making the walls of Jericho come tumbling down, about the shepherd boy David killing Goliath and conquering a great empire, and about Solomon's great wisdom and wealth. These legends were used by religious reformers to convince the people that strict monotheism would bring victory and prosperity.

But in its own way, the truth is as inspiring as the legends. The Israelites did not slaughter the Canaanites to take their land. Instead, living in small villages, supporting themselves with a primitive economy based on subsistence farming and herding, making many errors and missteps along the way, they helped to lay the foundation for several of the world's great religions while living on land that they had settled peacefully.

The Samaritan Book of Joshua

Chapter I

1. This is the book of days in which is found the chronicle from the time when Joshua son of Nun arrived in the land of Canaan to this day. In the year two thousand seven hundred four and ninety years after the creation of the world, in the twelfth month after the month of the death of the master of prophets, Moses son of Amram, the peace of the Lord be upon him,

2. At that time, the Lord said to Joshua son of Nun, the servant of Moses:

3. My servant Moses is dead, and now rise and cross this Jordan, you and all the children of Israel, to the land that I have given to them.

4. Every place that the sole of your foot travels on, I give to you, as I spoke to Moses,

5. From this desert and Lebanon and up to the great river, the Euphrates, all the land of the Hittites, and up to the great sea where the sun goes shall be your borders.

6. No man will take his stand before you all the days of your life. As I was with Moses, I will be with you. I will not slacken, and I will not leave.

7. Only be strong and very eager to observe and follow all the commandments of the Law that I commanded to Moses My servant. Do not deviate from it, not to the

right and not to the left, so that you will succeed in all that you go through.

8. And Joshua sat upon his seat.

9. And he called to the officers of the people and commanded them, saying,

10. Appoint the sons of Israel from the age of twenty years upward, appoint all to come out as an army in Israel. As Joshua commanded,

11. All the sons of Israel were appointed as an army, from the twenty-year-olds up to the fifty-year-olds, six hundred thousand and one thousand and seven hundred and thirty.

12. And the count of the tribe of the sons of Levi, from one month old upward, was three and twenty thousand.

13. And it happened after these things, Joshua son of Nun heard about the matter of the Canaanite nation.*

14. And he said to the Reubenites and the Gadites and to half the tribe of Manasseh,

15. Remember this word that Moses, the servant of the Lord, commanded you, saying:

16. The Lord your God bestowed upon you and gave to you this land.

17. Your wives and your little children and your herds will remain in this land, that Moses, the servant of God, has given you, this side of the Jordan,

18. And you will cross, battle-ready, in the presence of your brothers, the sons of Israel, all the mighty men of

* This verse is corrupt, and Gaster has tried to reconstruct it. He translated the Hebrew DBR into German "Wort" meaning "word," but here we translate it as "matter" (that is, the subject of the Canaanites). The Hebrew DBR could mean either, but "matter" seems to make more sense in context.

valor, and you will help them*

19. Until the Lord has given them rest and, like you, they also have inherited the land that the Lord your God has given them. Then crossing the Jordan, you will return to the land of your inheritance.

20. And they answered Joshua saying, We will do all that you commanded us, and we will go everywhere that you sent us. As we listened to everything from Moses, thus will we listen to you.

Chapter II

1. And Joshua son of Nun sent spies from the tribes to explore the land of Canaan,

2. And he commanded them to go to the city of Jericho and to know the number of inhabitants and those who joined them from the camps, and to return him word.

3. And they went and they came to the house of a harlot, and her name was Rahab, and they lay down there.

4. And someone told the king of Jericho, Behold, men come here this night from the sons of Israel to explore the land.

5. And the king of Jericho sent to Rahab saying, Send out the men who came to you, who came to your house, in order to explore all the land.

6. And the woman took the men, the spies, and hid them, and she said, Yes, they came to me, and I did not know where they were from,

7. And the gate was to be closed for the darkness,

* LFNI usually means "before," but based on the context, here, it seems to mean "in front of" or "in the presence of" rather than "at an earlier time than."

8. And the men went out in the darkness, and I do not know where they went. Pursue after them quickly, and you will get them.

9. And she brought them up to the roof and hid them under her flax stalks on the roof.

10. And the men pursued after them, the way of the Jordan on the fords, and they shut the gate after them after the pursuers went out.

11. And before they slept, she went up to them on the roof,

12. And she said to them, I know that the Lord, the God of your fathers, gave the land to you, and that we will fall before you, and that all the dwellers of the land are afraid of you,

13. For we have heard what the Lord did to the waters of the Red Sea before you when you came out from Egypt and what you did to the two kings of the Amorites, to Sichon and Og, that you destroyed them.

14. And we heard and our hearts dissolved and spirit no longer rose in a man before you, because the Lord your God He is the God in the heavens above and in the earth below.

15. And now please swear to me by the Lord, the God of your fathers, that I have acted kindly with you and you will also act kindly with the house of my father, and give to me a sign of truth,

16. And save the house of my father and protect all our souls from death.

17. And the men made a covenant with her about this matter, saying,

18. When the Lord, our God, gives us this land, we will do with you kindness and truth.

19. And she let them down on a rope through the window, for her house was at the wall, and at the wall she dwelt.

20. And she said to them, Go to the mountains, lest those who pursue after you harm you, and hide there in the mountain three days, until the pursuers return, and afterwards, go on your way.

21. And the men said to her, We are free of this oath that you made us swear

22. Unless you tie a scarlet cord to this window which you sent us down through, and you gather to yourself all the house of your father to this house. And she sent them, and they went.

23. And she tied a scarlet cord to the window.

24. And the spies returned,

25. And they came to Joshua son of Nun and told him all that had happened to them

26. And they spoke these things before him and before Eliezer the son of Aaron the priest, and before all the heads of the tribes of Israel.

Chapter III

1. And Joshua rose in the morning, and they traveled from Shittim and came to the Jordan, he and all the sons of Israel, and they camped before they crossed.

2. And it happened at the end of three days, the officers passed near the campsite,

3. And they commanded the people, saying, When you see the ark of the covenant of the Lord your God and the Levite priests carrying it, you shall set out from your place and you shall go after it,

4. But there shall be a distance between you and between it of about two thousand cubits. Do not come closer to it so that you will know the way you are going on, for you have not crossed on that way yesterday or the day before.

5. And Joshua son of Nun said to the people, Sanctify yourselves, for tomorrow the Lord your God will do wonders among you.

6. And Joshua son of Nun said the the priests, saying, Take the ark of the covenant of the Lord and pass before the people. And they took the ark of the covenant of the Lord and went before the people.

7. And the priests sang to the Lord, saying,

8. Be He praised Who was before all.

9. Be He praised Whose glory is above all.

10. Be He praised Who was before all time.

11. Be He praised Who created all time.

12. Be He praised Who has all things under His will.

13. Be He praised Whom there is nothing like.

14. Be He praised Who gave us manna and all things.*

15. Be He praised Who made all things.

16. Be praised the God of Gods and Lord of Lords.

17. Be He praised under Whose word are the heaven and the earth and the sea.

18. Be He praised Who created day and night.†

19. Be He praised Who created all created things.

20. Be He praised Who worked wonders.

* This line is corrupt, and the translation is speculative.

† This verse uses a different word for "praise." The others use the root HLL. This uses the root ShBH. This is probably a corruption of the text.

21. Be He praised Who revealed the signs and the miracles.

22. There is no other apart from Him.

23. And there is no glory but His glory, no domination but His domination, no rule but His rule, no holiness but His holiness. Sanctified is His name, and blessed is His name forever.

24. And the Lord said to Joshua, This day, I will begin to aggrandize you in the eyes of all the people of Israel, so that they will know that, as I was with Moses my servant, so I will be with you.

25. And now, command the priests carrying the ark of the covenant of the Lord,

26. When you come to the edge of the water of the Jordan, stand at the Jordan.

27. And Joshua said this to the priests carrying the ark of the covenant of the Lord,

28. And they did that which the Lord commanded King Joshua son of Nun.

29. And the priests went when the cloud lifted, and they were distant from the camp, as King Joshua commanded them.

30. And Joshua son of Nun commanded the people, saying,

31. Take ye twelve men, one man from each tribe,

32. And it will happen that, when the soles of the feet of the priests carrying the ark of the covenant of the Lord rest in the water of the Jordan, the water of the Jordan will be cut. The water of the Jordan from above will stand in one heap.

33. And it happened, when the bearers of the ark of the

covenant of the Lord came to the Jordan, and their feet were wet at the edge of the Jordan, and the Jordan was full all the way up its banks, all the days of harvest,

34. And the water from above stood and rose in one heap,

35. And the water dried up and was cut off.

36. And the priests carrying the ark of the covenant of the Lord stood on dry land in the midst of the Jordan.

37. And the priests and all the people of Israel crossed on dry land until all the nation finished crossing.

Chapter IV

1. And Joshua son of Nun called upon the twelve men whom he had appointed from the sons of Israel,

2. And he said to them, Cross before the ark of the covenant of the Lord your God in the midst of the Jordan and each man lift one stone on his shoulder to the number of the tribes of the children of Israel

3. In order that this may be a sign to you of your crossing. For when your children ask you tomorrow saying, what are those stones to you?

4. You will say to them that the waters of the Jordan were divided before the ark of the covenant of the Lord, and these stones are for a memorial for the children of Israel forever.

5. And the children of Israel did what Joshua son of Nun commanded them, thus they did.

6. And they carried twelve stones out of the midst of the Jordan, and they placed them.

7. And Joshua son of Nun raised twelve stones in the midst of the Jordan, in the place of the feet of the priests

who carried the ark of the covenant of the Lord, and they were there.

8. In that day, the Lord aggrandized Joshua son of Nun in the eyes of all the congregation of the people of Israel.

9. When the priests who carried the ark of the covenant of the Lord came up from the midst of the Jordan, the waters of the Jordan returned to their place.

10. And the people came up from the Jordan on the tenth day of the first month.

Chapter V

1. On that day, Joshua son of Nun stood and sang the song of Moses, which Moses, lord of the prophets, and the children of Israel sang at the Red sea, and all the children of Israel with him.

2. And after all this he said,

3. Praised be Who created the creation.

4. Praised be Who created the heavens and the lands.

5. Praised be Who is one.

6. Praised be Who is the God of spirits.

7. Praised be Who has no equals.

8. Praised be Who has done the wonders.

9. Praised be Who has revealed the signs.

10. Praised be Whose thought you cannot know.

11. Praised be Who has discovered all that has been discovered.

12. Praised be Who encompasses all places.

13. Praised be Who lights the darkness.

14. Praised be Whom all places do not encompass.

15. Praised be Who moves the stars in the heavens.

16. You are God, and there is none like You.

17. You are the maker of all works and images and creatures and spirits.

18. Blessed be Your great name for ever and ever, blessed be the name of Your holiness forever. There is no* God but One.

19. And Joshua son of Nun was great in the eyes of all the congregation of Israel, like the greatness of the lord of prophets, Moses son of Amram, peace be upon him.

20. And the heads of the nation raised up the twelve stones in the place Gilgal as a memorial of what the Lord did with his people the children of Israel at the time when they crossed the Jordan.

21. And the king of Damascus heard of the children of Israel's crossing of the Jordan and of its drying up at the time when they crossed it and of its returning as it was before at the time when they came out from it,

22. And fear and dread fell upon them.

23. And the Lord said to Joshua son of Nun, See, I have brought dread of you and fear of you before all the nations.

24. And I have taken away from you and from your nation every plague.

25. And Joshua son of Nun called the name of that place Gilgal.

* The text uses the Aramaic word LIT to mean "there is no" rather than the common Hebrew word EN, implying either that this prayer is a later Samaritan addition to the Israelite source text or that the Aramaic word is an error introduced by a later scribe.

Chapter VI

1. And the cloud lifted up from over the children of Israel on the first month,[*] the beginning of the year of Shmita[†] and of Jubilee[‡] for the children of Israel.

2. Which was the year two thousand seven hundred four and ninety years from the creation of the world.[§]

3. In this month, on its fourteenth day, in the evening, they made the sacrifice of Passover in the plains of Jericho,

4. And they ate matzos seven days from the grain of the land,

5. And the manna stopped on that day of their eating the grain of the land, and there was no more,

6. And they ate of the produce of the land that year.

7. And it happened that when Joshua son of Nun was at Jericho, he raised his eyes and saw, and behold, a man was standing opposite him and a drawn sword was in his hand.

8. And Joshua son of Nun went to him and said to him, Do you go with us or with our enemies?

9. And he said to him, I am captain of the host of the Lord. Now I come.

10. And Joshua son of Nun fell on his face and prostrated himself

* In the Samaritan calendar, the first month is Nisan, the month when Passover occurs. Among Jews, the first month is sometimes considered to be Nisan and sometimes Tishri, when Rosh Hashannah occurs.

† The seventh year of the seven-year agricultural cycle, when the land was required to lay fallow.

‡ The year that follows seven of the seven-year agricultural cycles.

§ Once again, the Samaritan book emphasizes chronology. The first three verses of this chapter are not in the Biblical book.

11. And he said to him, What does my lord speak to his servant?
12. Take off your shoes from on your feet, for the place you are standing on is holy. And Joshua did so.

Chapter VII

1. And the angel of the Lord said* to Joshua son of Nun, Thus says the Lord, See, I give into your hand this city and its king and the mighty men of valor.
2. And you shall circle the city, all the men of war going around the city one time. Thus you shall do to the city six days.
3. And the priests carrying the ark of the covenant shall be in front of the people and in their hands the shofars.†
4. And on the seventh day, you shall circle around the city seven times. The seventh time, the priests shall blow the shofars.
5. And when you hear the voice of the shofar, all the nation will shout a great shout and will say, The Lord is mighty in war. The Lord is his name. And the walls of the city will fall and the people will go up, each man against it.
6. And Joshua son of Nun called the priests and said to them, Carry the ark of the covenant of the Lord, and seven priests carry seven ram's horn shofars before the ark of the covenant of the Lord.

* In the Biblical book, the angel appears for no reason and the Lord speaks directly to Joshua in the verse that is equivalent to this one (Jos 6:2). In the Samaritan book, more reasonably, the angel appears and speaks to Joshua.

† Rams horns used as trumpets.

7. And he said to the people, Circle the city, and the men at arms pass before the ark of the covenant of the Lord.

8. And it happened that when Joshua spoke to the people, the priests passed and blew the shofars,

9. And the ark of the covenant of the Lord went after them.

10. And Joshua commanded the people, saying, Do not shout and do not make your voices heard until the day when the priests say to you to shout, and then shout.

11. And the ark of the congregation circled the city once, and they went to the camp and lodged in the camp.

12. And Joshua son on Nun rose in the morning, and the priests took the ark of the covenant of the Lord,

13. And the priests blew the shofars.

14. And they circled the city six days, once each day.

15. And it happened on the seventh day, and they rose at dawn, and they circled the city seven times,

16. And the seventh time the priests blew the trumpet and all the people shouted, The Lord is a mighty man of war. The Lord is His name. And Joshua said to the people, Shout, for the Lord has given you this city.

17. And this city will be devoted* to the Lord, it and all who are in it. Only Rahab the harlot will live, she and all who are with her in her house, because she hid the messengers whom we sent to spy on this city.

18. You shall observe this curse, lest you put this curse on the camp of Israel and upset it.

* Herem is a hard word to translate. It can mean something devoted to the Lord, or something under a curse, or something to be destroyed. Here, it is translated both as "devoted" and as "under a curse."

19. And all the articles of silver and articles of gold and brass and iron are devoted to the Lord.*

20. Then the people shouted a great shout, and the wall fell down, and the people went up to the city, each man against it, and they took the city.

21. And they destroyed everything that was in the city, from man to woman to sheep and donkeys.

22. And to the two men who had spied the land, Joshua son of Nun said, Go to the house of the woman and take out from there the woman and all that is hers, as you swore to her.

23. And they went to the house, and they took out Rahab and her father and her mother and her brothers and all her family.

24. And they burned the city with fire and all that was in it.

25. And Joshua swore at that time saying, Accursed be the man before the Lord who rises up and builds this city, Jericho.

26. And the Lord was with Joshua son of Nun, and his fame was in all the land.

Chapter VIII

1. And a man of the children of Israel went from house to house in Jericho, and he took a golden idol and a gold-

---

* In the Bible, Jos 6:19 includes the explanation: "But all the silver, and gold, and vessels of brass and iron, are holy unto the Lord; they shall come into the treasury of the Lord," and Jos 6:24 says, "And they burnt the city with fire, and all that was therein; only the silver, and the gold, and the vessels of brass and of iron, they put into the treasury of the house of the Lord."

en wedge of the weight of two thousand two hundred shekels.*

2. And afterwards, the anger of the Lord was upon the children of Israel.

3. And Joshua son of Nun sent from the people three thousand men from Jericho to Ai, and the men of Ai drove out the three thousand men that Joshua son of Nun had sent.

4. And they fled from before the men of Ai, for they had killed among them six and thirty men.

5. And they returned to Joshua son of Nun, to the camp.

6. And Joshua rent his clothes, and he fell on his face to the earth before the ark of the congregation, and all the elders of the children of Israel with him.

7. And Joshua said, Oh Lord, my lord, why have you brought this people across the Jordan to give us into the hands of the Amorites to destroy us?

8. What will I say when the children of Israel have gone back before their enemies?

9. And all the dwellers of the land of Canaan will hear and surround us to destroy us from the land.

10. And the Lord said to Joshua son of Nun, Why do fall on your nose?

11. Rise up, for Israel has sinned and has taken from the devoted thing.

12. Go to the people, and let the man who took from the devoted thing be burned in fire, for he has made an abomination in Israel.

* Jos 7:1 gives the name of the man but does not specify what he took: "But the children of Israel committed a trespass concerning the devoted thing; for Achan, the son of Carmi, the son of Zabdi, the son of Zerah, of the tribe of Judah, took of the devoted thing; and the anger of the Lord was kindled against the children of Israel."

13. And Joshua the son of Nun rose and gathered all the camp of the children of Israel to the opening of the of the tent of meeting before Eliezer the son of Aaron the priest, with rows of stones on his breastplate and the Urim and the Thumim.

14. And he brought out the names of the tribes, tribe by tribe, and the outcome was from the tribe of Judah. And he brought out the names of the families of Judah,

15. And the outcome discovered the family of Zarhi. And he brought out the names of the family of Zarhi,

16. And the outcome discovered the house of Zabdi. And he brought out the men of the house of Zabdi,

17. And the stone darkened on the name of Ailan.

18. And he was Ailan the son of Carmi, the son of Zabdi, of the tribe of Judah.

19. And Joshua son of Nun said to Ailan, Son, my son, know that the Creator of the heavens and the earth knows all hidden things and all redeemed things, and nothing can be concealed from Him. Tell me what you did, before this people. Do not hide anything from us.

20. And Ailan answered Joshua son of Nun,

21. The Lord is the righteous one, and I am the wicked one. And he said, I have sinned against the Lord, God of Israel, and I have done this.

22. And Joshua son of Nun sent messengers, and they ran to the tent, and behold this idol and this wedge were hidden in his tent, and the silver was under it.

23. And they brought them to Joshua son of Nun, and he restored them before the Lord.

24. And Joshua took the idol and the wedge and the silver

and Ailan and his sons and his daughters and all the souls of his house and all that was his

25. And all the assembled congregation of the children of Israel stoned them with stones and burned them with fire

26. And they raised above them a great heap of stones to this day, and the Lord relented upon the people, and He returned from the wrath of his anger.

Chapter IX

1. And the Lord said to Joshua son of Nun, Do not fear, and do not dismay.

2. Take the men of war, and rise, go up to Ai, for I have given into your hand the king of Ai and all his people and all his land.

3. And Joshua son of Nun chose from the people three thousand men and sent them by night.

4. And Joshua son of Nun commanded them, saying, See, you shall lie in ambush at the city, behind the city, do not distance yourselves much, and all of you be ready,

5. And I and all of the people who are with me will come close to the city,

6. And it will happen that the people of the city will come out against us, and we will flee from before them,

7. And you will rise and come out from your ambush and will take the city, and the Lord will give it to you, into your hands.

8. And they did as Joshua son of Nun commanded them.

9. And the Lord gave it into the hand of Israel, and they burned with fire it and everything that was in it, as the Lord commanded Joshua.

10. And this is the city that is before Mt. Gerizim, whose name is Bethel, on the east side.

11. And Joshua went to the city of Luz, which is in Mt. Gerizim, which is Bethel, and he killed all the people who dwelt in it, and there was not any remnant of them that remained.

12. And Joshua son of Nun commanded the people, saying they shall travel from Gilgal

13. And they shall camp in Elon Moreh, which is near the city of Shechem, and they pitched the tent of meeting there.

14. And Joshua son of Nun built an altar of stones on Mt. Gerizim,* which is Bethel, as Moses commanded the children of Israel according to the word of the Lord, unhewn stones.

15. And there went up from it burnt offerings and peace offerings.

16. And fire came out from the Lord and consumed what was on the altar. And the children of Israel rejoiced and multiplied songs and praises to the Lord, their God, who chose them from all the nations.

17. And the leader of the leaders of the priests, Eliezer son of Aaron the priest, wrote on the stones all the words of the Law of Moses, clearly and well, according to what Moses commanded in the book of the Law, saying,

18. And it will be, when you cross over the Jordan, you shall raise these stones, as I command you today, on Mt. Gerizim, and you will plaster them with lime.

19. And they set it up on Mt. Gerizim, as the Lord commanded Moses.

* Jos 8:30 says he built the altar on Mt. Ebal.

20. And Joshua son of Nun gathered all of the assembly of the congregation of the children of Israel near Mt. Gerizim Bethel, and they gathered around the mountain on the four sides.

21. And the Levite priests came near and they read all the words of the Law aloud.

22. And after this, they divided the tribes of Reuben, Gad, Asher, Dan, Zebulon, and Naphtali, and they went and stood on Mt. Ebal.*

23. And the tribes of Simeon, Levi, Judah, Isachar, Joseph, and Benjamin went and stood on Mt. Gerizim.

24. And the ark of the covenant of the Lord was with them, and the Levite priests carried it.

25. And before them, the high priest Eliezer the son of Aaron the priest, peace be upon him, and his son Phinehas and his brother Itamar, peace be upon them, and all the elders of Israel and their judges.

26. And the great ones of the priests blessed on Mt. Gerizim Bethel, in the name of the Lord, the Holy One, all of the assembly of the children of Israel.

27. And they read all the words of the blessing of God over them, and they blessed them, and the glory of God appeared upon the ark of the covenant.

28. And all the people saw and rejoiced and fell on their faces. And after this, the Levites turned their faces to the side of Mt. Ebal.

29. And they read all the words of the curses written in this book of the Law, as the Lord commanded Moses.

* In Deut 27, Moses commands this ceremony on Mt. Gerizim and Mt. Ebal, blessing the Israelites if they obey the Law and cursing them if they disobey. The Biblical Book of Joshua does not include the specifics of this ceremony.

30. And it happened after these things, and the people went, each man to his tent.

31. And Joshua son of Nun commanded, and they buried the bones of Joseph in the portion of the field which our father Jacob bought from the hand of the sons of Hamor, father of Shechem, for a hundred pieces of money.

32. And it happened in Shechem, in Elon Moreh, in the place where Jacob built an altar and called its name El Elohei Israel.

Chapter X

1. And it happened after these things, all the people and the nations heard that Joshua son of Nun and his people, the children of Israel, captured the city of Jericho and Ai and the city of Luz

2. And the city of Shechem and all of their villages, and they were very afraid.

3. And the inhabitants of the villages that were near those cities, and of them the inhabitants of Gibeon, came to Joshua son of Nun and to Eliezer the priest, and to all the elders of the children of Israel with guile.

4. And they came with worn-out sackcloth

5. And with old sandals and patches on their feet, and worn clothing upon them, and all the bread provisioning them was dry and moldy.

6. And they came to Joshua son of Nun and they said to him and to Eliezer son of Aaron and to all the heads of the people, We come to you from a distant land, and now, make a covenant with us.

7. And Joshua son of Nun and Eliezer son of Aaron the priest and the elders of the people said to them, Perhaps

you live among us, and how can we make a covenant with you?

8. And they said to them, We, your servants, are from a far country. And they said to them, Who are you and where do you come from?

9. And they said, Your servants came from a very far country for the sake of the Lord, your God, for we have surely heard everything that the Lord did in Egypt

10. And everything that He did to the two kings, the kings of the Amorites, who are across the Jordan, to Sihon king of Heshbon, and to Og king of Bashan, at Ashtaroth in Edrei.

11. And the elders and all the dwellers in our land said to us, saying, Take in your hand provisions for the road, and go to call them, and say to them, we are your servants and now make a covenant with us.

12. This is the bread with which we provisioned ourselves from our houses on the day when we left to go to you, and now it is dry and moldy.

13. And these are the wineskins which we filled when they were new, and behold, they are broken. And these our clothes and shoes are worn out from the very long road.

14. And the men took their provisions as evidence, and they did not ask the word of the Lord.

15. And Joshua son of Nun made peace with them, and made a covenant with them for their lives, and the leaders of the congregation made an oath to them.

16. And it happened, at the end of three days after they made a covenant with them, they heard that they were near to them and they dwelt near them.

17. And the children of Israel travelled and came to their cities on the third day, and their cities were Gibeon, and Kizah, and Shitah, and Kiriath Jearim.

18. And the children of Israel did not attack them, because Joshua son of Nun, and Eliezer son of Aaron the priest, and the leaders of the congregation swore to them by the Lord, God of Israel, and all the congregation murmured against the leaders.

19. And all of the leaders said to all of the congregation, We swore to them by the Lord, God of Israel, and now, we cannot touch them.

20. Thus will we do to them. We will let them live, and there will not be wrath upon us on account of the oath that we swore to them.

21. And the leaders said to them, They will live, and they will be choppers of wood and drawers of water for all of the congregation. Thus the leaders spoke to them.

22. And Joshua son of Nun called them and spoke to them, saying, Why did you deceive us, saying you were very far from us, when you dwell near us?

23. And now you are accursed, and your work will never be ended, chopping wood and drawing water for the house of God.

24. And they answered Joshua, saying, Because your servants were told that the Lord, your God, commanded Moses, his servant, to give you all the land and commanded you to destroy all the dwellers in the land before you, we were afraid and we did this thing.

25. And now, here we are in your hand. Do what is good and right in your eyes to do with us.

26. And Joshua took them out of the hands of the children of Israel and did not kill them.
27. And after this, Joshua made them choppers of wood and drawers of water for the altar of the Lord in the chosen place, Mt. Gerizim.

Chapter XI

1. And it happened when the king of Jebus* heard that the dwellers in Gibeon made peace with Israel and were living among them,
2. And he was very afraid, because it was a big city like one of the cities of his kingdom, and because it was bigger than Ai, and all its men were mighty.
3. And the king of Jebus sent to the king of Hebron and to the king of Jarmuth, the king of Lachish, and the king of Eglon, saying,
4. Come up to me, and help me, and strike Gibeon, for they have made peace with Joshua son of Nun and with the people of the children of Israel.
5. And the five kings of the Amorites gathered together and came up, the king of Jebus, and the king of Hebron, and the king of Jarmuth, and the king of Lachish, and the king of Eglon, and they camped at Gibeon, and they made war against it.
6. And the men of Gibeon sent to Joshua son of Nun, saying, Do not withhold your hands from your servants. Come up to us quickly and save us and help us, for all the kings of the Amorites who dwell in the hill country have gathered against us.

* Jos 10:1 specifies "Adoni-zedek king of Jerusalem." Jebus is the name the Bible generally uses for Jerusalem when the Israelites arrived.

7. And Joshua son of Nun rose up from Mt. Gerizim Bethel, the chosen place, he and all the people of war of his people, and all the mighty men of valor

8. And the Lord said to Joshua, Do not fear, for I have given them into your hand. Not a man of them will stand before you.

9. And Joshua came to them suddenly,

10. And the Lord confused them before Israel, and they slaughtered them with a great slaughter in Gibeon, and they chased them on the road going up to Beth Horon

11. And smote them as far as Azekah and Makkedah, which is west of Bethel, which is Mt. Gerizim.

12. Then Joshua spoke before the Lord on that day, when the Lord put the Amorites before the children of Israel,

13. And the Lord gave the kings of the Amorites on that day into the hands of the children of Israel

14. And they slew them with a very great slaughter.

15. And Joshua son of Nun and all the children of Israel, his people, returned to Bethel, to Mt. Gerizim, the chosen place.

16. And those five kings went away and hid in a cave in Makkedah.

17. And someone told Joshua, saying, The five kings are to be found hidden in a cave in Makkedah.

18. And Joshua said, Roll big stones to the mouth of the cave, and station men on it to watch it.

19. And as for you, do not stand. Pursue your enemies and smite their stragglers. Do not let them come to their cities, for the Lord, your God, has given them into your hands.

20. And it happened, when Joshua and the children of Israel finished killing them with a very great slaughter until they were consumed, the survivors who survived among them came to their fortified cities.

21. And all of the people returned to the camp, to Joshua son of Nun at Makkadah in peace. No one moved his tongue against any man of the children of Israel.

22. And Joshua said, Open the mouth of the cave, and bring out to me those five kings from the cave.

23. And they did so and brought those five kings from the cave: the king of Jebus, the king of Hebron, the king of Jarmuth, the king of Lachish, and the king of Eglon.

24. And it happened, when they brought those kings to Joshua, Joshua called to all the men of Israel, and he said to the leaders of the men of war who had gone with him, Come near and put your feet on the necks of these kings. And they came near and put their feet on their necks.

25. And Joshua said to them, Do not be afraid and do not be alarmed. Be strong and be courageous, for thus the Lord will do to all your enemies whom you make war against.

26. And after that, Joshua arose, and he killed them, and he hung them on five trees. And it happened that they hung on the trees until evening.

27. And it happened at the time when the sun set, Joshua commanded, and they took them down from the trees, and they took them to the cave where they had hidden, and they put big stones on the mouth of the cave, closed until this day.

28. And Joshua captured Makkedah on that day, and he smote them with the edge of the sword, and he destroyed

its king, and of all the souls in it, he did not let any remain. And he did to the king of Makkedah as he had done to the king of Jericho.

29. And Joshua and all who were with him passed from Makkedah to Libnah.

30. And the Lord also gave it and its king into the hand of Israel. And they smote it with the edge of the sword. And of all the souls who were in it, he did not let any remain. And he did to its king as he had done to the king of Jericho.

31. And Joshua and all Israel with him passed from Libnah to Lachish, and they camped at it and they made war on it.

32. And the Lord gave Lachish into the hand of Israel. And they took it on the second day. And they smote it with the edge of the sword and all the souls who were in it, as they had done to Libnah.

33. Then Haram, king of Gezer, came up to rescue Lachish from the hand of Israel, and Joshua and his people smote them until none of them remained.

34. And Joshua and all Israel with him passed from Lachish to Eglon, and they camped at it and they made war on it.

35. And they captured it that day and smote it with the edge of the sword, and they destroyed all the souls in it on that day, as they had done to Lachish.

36. And Joshua and all Israel with him went up from Eglon to Hebron, and they made war on it.

37. And they captured it and smote it with the edge of the sword, and its king, and its towns, and all the souls that were in it. No remnant survived. As they had done to Eglon, they destroyed it and all the souls in it.

38. And Joshua and all of Israel with him turned to Debirah, and they made war on it.

39. And they captured it and smote it with the edge of the sword, and they destroyed its king, and all its towns, and all the souls in it. No remnant survived. As he had done to Hebron and as he had done to Libnah and its king, so he did to Debirah and its king.

40. And Joshua smote all the land, the Negev and the hill country and the plains, and the slopes. And all their kings and every soul he destroyed, no remnant survived, as the Lord, God of Israel, commanded.

41. And Joshua went up from Kadesh Barnea to Gaza, and all the land of Goshen up to Gibeon.

42. And Joshua captured all those kings and all their lands at once, for the Lord, God of Israel, fought for Israel.

43. And it happened that Joshua son of Nun came out from fighting with them at the beginning of the eighth month, and he returned to the chosen place on the first month of the second year after the children of Israel crossed into the land of Canaan.

44. And Joshua son of Nun, before returning to the chosen place, stayed in Gilgal, he and all the people of war, by themselves for seven days.

45. And it happened, on the evening of the seventh day, Joshua son of Nun and all the people of war who were with him, washed their flesh, and they purified themselves from uncleanness in the water used for impurity on the third day and on the seventh day, and they washed their clothing in water, and they were purified.

46. And all the children of Israel made, in that month, the Passover sacrifice, at the appointed time in the chosen

place, Mt. Gerizim Bethel, with very abundant joy and happiness.

Chapter XII

1. And it happened that, when Jabin king of Hazor heard of it, he sent to Jobab king of Madon, and to the king of Shamron and to the king of Achshaph,
2. And to the kings who were north, in the hill country and in the plain, south of Chinnereth, and in the lowland and in Naphoth-Dor at the sea,
3. To the Canaanites in the east on the sea, and the Amorites and the Hittites and the Perizzites and the Jebusites in the hill country, and the Hivites at the foot of Hermon in the land of Mizpah.
4. And they went out, them and all their armies with them, abundant as sand that is at the edge of the sea, and very abundant horses and chariots.
5. And all those kings gathered and came and camped and came together at the waters of Merom to war with Israel.
6. And the Lord said to Joshua, Do not fear before them, for tomorrow at this time, I will have given all of them, slain before Israel. You shall lame their horses, and you shall burn their chariots with fire.
7. And Joshua and all the people of war with him fell upon them suddenly at the waters of Merom.
8. And the Lord gave them into the hand of Israel, and they struck them and they chased them as far as Misrephoth-Mayim and as far as the valley of Mizpah on the east, and they struck them so no survivor remained of them.

9. And Joshua did to them what the Lord said to him. He lamed their horses, and he burned their chariots with fire.

10. And Joshua returned at that time and captured Hazor and struck its king with the sword, for Hazor was the head of all of those kingdoms.

11. And they struck down all the souls who were in it with the edge of the sword and destroyed them. Not any soul was left, and he burned Hazor with fire.

12. And Joshua the son of Nun captured all the cities of those kings and their kings, and struck them down with the edge of the sword and destroyed them, as Moses, the servant of the Lord, had commanded.

13. Only the Israelites did not burn all the cities that were on high places, except that Joshua burned only Hazor.

14. And the children of Israel took all the spoils of those cities and the animals in them; only they struck down all the people in them with the edge of the sword until they destroyed them. Not a soul survived.

15. As the Lord had commanded Moses, his servant, so Moses had commanded Joshua son of Nun. And so Joshua did. He did not lack anything from all that the Lord commanded Moses.

16. And Joshua took all this land, all the hill country, and all the south, and all the land of Goshen, and the valley, and the plain, and the hill country of Israel, and its plain, and its desert valley, and the hill country of Israel and its plain.

17. From the hill country that rises toward Seir up to the valley of Lebanon at the foot of Mt. Hermon, and he captured all of their kings.

18. And he struck them and killed them.

19. There was not a city that made peace with the Israelites. Except for the Hivites dwelling in Gibeon, they took them all in war.

20. For it was from the Lord to strengthen their hearts when war befell Israel in order that they destroy them and not have mercy on their lives but kill them, as the Lord had commanded Moses.

21. And Joshua came at that time and cut off the Anakim* from the hill country, from Hebron, from Debir and from Anak. Joshua son of Nun destroyed them with their cities.

22. The Anakim were not left in the land of the children of Israel, they remained only in Gaza, in Gath and in Ashdod.

23. And Joshua took all the land, as the Lord had spoken to Moses. And Joshua gave it as an inheritance to Israel, in their divisions, to their tribes. And the land quieted from its war.

Chapter XIII

1. And it happened after these things that Joshua son of Nun and Caleb son of Jephunneh undertook to make a place to set up the dwelling place of the Lord in the chosen place, Mt. Gerizim Bethel, as the Lord has commanded to Moses his servant.

2. And they cut the hill which was at the top of Mt. Gerizim whose name was called the Eternal Hill.

3. And they anointed it and raised the dwelling place on it, the Holy of Holies, and Joshua son of Nun built a courtyard on that mountain, on the north side.

* A supposed race of giants descended from Anak.

4. And the children of Israel camped, each man in his place, and the Levites each man in the place that was his, and Israel dwelt securely.

5. And it happened that Joshua son of Nun appointed one day in every seven days with the High Priest, Eliezer son of Aaron the priest,

6. And one day with the wise men of the children of Israel and the elders,

7. And one day with the heads of the people and their officers,

8. And one day to his own activities, and to watching the affairs of the congregation and to judging the people three days.

9. And Joshua son of Nun built according to the word of the Lord, and he finished it on the head of Mt. Gerizim Bethel, for it was the place that the Lord had chosen for His name to dwell there.

10. And he put in it the tent of meeting and the ark of testimony and the covering veil and all the altars and all the vessels of the tabernacle, each one on its base.

11. At that time, he gathered together all the people, all their leaders and their officers and their judges,

12. And he portioned the land to the nine tribes and the half tribe by casting lots, to their families, as the Lord had commanded by the hand of Moses his servant.

13. For the tribe of the sons of Reuben and the tribe of the sons of the Gadites and the half tribe of Manasseh had taken their inheritance that Moses the servant of God had given them across the Jordan to the east

14. From Aroer, which is on the banks of the Arnon River, and the city in the middle of the river valley and all the valley of Medebah to Dibon,

15. And all the cities of Sihon king of the Amorites, who reigned in Heshbon, to the border of the sons of Ammon.

16. And Gilead, and the territory of the Geshurites and the Maacathites, and all the hill country of Herrnon, and all Bashan up to Salchah,

17. All the kingdom of Og in Bashan, who reigned in Ashtaroth and Edrei. He was the remnant of the Rephaim,* and Moses struck them and expelled them.

18. But the children of Israel did not expel the Geshurites and the Maacbatites, and the Geshurites and the Maacbatites dwelt among the children of Israel.

19. Only to the tribe of Levi he did not give an inheritance. The sacrifices of the Lord, God of Israel, are its inheritance, as He said to it.

20. And Moses gave to the tribe of the sons of Reuben, to its families,

21. And their boundaries are from Aroer, which is on the banks of the Arnon River, and the city in the middle of the river valley and all the valley, and all Medebah,

22. Heshbon, and all its cities that are in the valley before Dibon, and Bamoth-baal, and Beth-baalmon, and Jahzah, and Kedemoth, and Mephaath,

23. And Kiriathaim, and Sibmah, and Zereth-Hashachar in Mt. Amek,

24. And Beth-peor, and the slopes of Pisgah, and Beth-Haishimoth,

25. And all the cities of the plain, and all the kingdom of Sihon king of the Amorites, who dwelt in Heshbon, whom Moses had slain, him and all the leaders of Mid-

* Another supposed race of giants.

ian, Evi, and Rekem, and Zur, and Hur, and Reba, the leaders of Sihon who dwelt in the land.

26. And Balaam the son of Beor, the soothsayer, they slew with the sword, among those slain by them.

27. And the border of the sons of Reuben was the Jordan, and this is the border of the inheritance of the sons of Reuben for their families and cities and villages.

28. And Moses gave to the tribe of the sons of Gad to their families,

29. And their border was Jaaser, and all the cities of Gilead, and half the land of the sons of Ammon to Aroer, which is before Rabbah,

30. And from Heshbon to Rammat Mizpeh and Botnim, and from Mahanaim to the border of Debir,

31. And in the valley of Beth Haram and Beth Nimrah and Succoth and Zaphon, the rest of the kingdom of Sihon king of Heshbon, the Jordan, and a border up to the end of the Sea of Chinnereth, beyond the Jordan on the east.

32. This is the inheritance of the sons of Gad for their families and cities and villages.

33. And Moses gave to the half tribe of Manasseh, and it was for the half tribe of Manasseh for their families,

34. And the border was from Mahanaim up to Bashan, all the kingdom of Og, the king of Bashan, and all the villages of Jair, which are in Bashan, sixty cities,

35. And half of Gilead, and Ashtaroth, and Edrei, cities of the kingdom of Og in Bashan, to the sons of Machir, the son of Manasseh, to half of the sons of Machir to their families.

36. These are what Moses gave for an inheritance in the plains of Moab beyond the Jordan, east of Jericho.

37. And to the tribe of the Levites, Moses did not give an inheritance. The Lord, the God of Israel, is their inheritance, as he spoke to them.*

Chapter XIV

1. And these are what the children of Israel inherited in the land of Canaan, as Eleazar the priest and Joshua the son of Nun and the heads of the fathers of the tribes of the children of Israel distributed them.
2. They received them by lot, as the Lord commanded by the hand of Moses for the nine and a half tribes.
3. For Moses had given an inheritance to the two and a half tribes beyond the Jordan, and did not give an inheritance to the Levites among them.
4. For the children of Joseph were two tribes, namely Manasseh and Ephraim, and he did not give the Levites a portion of the land as an inheritance, except cities to dwell in, with their plots for their flocks and their property.
5. As the Lord commanded Moses, so did the children of Israel, and divided the land.
6. And the lot was to the tribe of the children of Judah to their families.
7. And its east side was the Sea of Chinnereth.†
8. And its west side was boundary of the inheritance of the tribe of the children of Simeon.
9. And its south side was the desert and the boundary of

* This verse repeats 12:19 with a minor variation, a corruption in the manuscript. The verse obviously belongs here and was added at 12:19 by mistake.

† This is a scribal error. The eastern border of Judah was the Dead Sea (also called the Salt Sea), not the Sea of Chinnereth (also called the Sea of Galillee).

Egypt.

10. And its north side was the boundary of the inheritance of the tribe of children of Benjamin, Jebus, and its towns.

11. And the lot was to the tribe of the children of Dan to their families; and their inheritance was to the side of the city of Kiriath Arba, which is the city of Hebron, and all its towns.*

12. And the lot was to the tribe of the children of Simeon to their families; on the east side was the inheritance of the tribe of the children of Judah,

13. And the west side was the sea, and the south side was the border of Egypt,

14. And the north side was the inheritance of the tribe of sons of Judah, and Gaza and all its towns, and Beersheba, and as far as the Jordan.

15. And the border to the the tribe of the children of Benjamin to their families; the east side was Jebus and all its towns eastward as far as the valley of the Jordan. And on the west side was the border of Kiriath Jearim and the inheritance of the tribe of the children of Dan.

16. And on the south was the inheritance of the tribe of the children of Judah, and on the north was the inheritance of the tribe of the children of Ephraim.

17. And the west side of the tribe of the children of Dan was the sea, and the east side was the inheritance of the tribe of the children of Benjamin.

18. And on the north was the inheritance of the tribe of the children of Ephraim, and on the south was the in-

* The manuscript is obviously corrupt. Verse 11 should be immediately before verse 17. "To the side of" seems to have been added by mistake.

heritance of the tribe of the children of Judah. So the inheritance of Benjamin and the inheritance of the tribe of Dan were matching, east and west.

19. The first in the hill country, and in it Jebus up to the Jordan, and the second from the side of the sea, and in it Philistines and Zorah.

20. And the lot was to the tribe of the children of Ephraim to their families, east from the side of the Jordan river from the border of Benjamin to the border of the tribe the sons of Manasseh,

21. And on the west side from the Salt Sea* to the border of the tribe of the children of Dan.

22. And on the south side the inheritance of the tribe of the children of Dan and the tribe of the children of Benjamin,

23. And on the north the inheritance of the half tribe of Manasseh,

24. And in this lot is the city of Shechem and the city of Samaria and all their towns.

25. And the lot was to the half tribe of Manasseh: on the east side, the Jordan River between the boundary of the tribe of the sons of Ephraim and the boundary of the tribe of Issachar, and on the west side, the sea up to Mt. Carmel,

26. And on the south side, the inheritance of the tribe of the children of Ephraim,

27. And on the north side, the inheritance of the tribe of the children of Zebulun and the tribe of the children of Issachar,

28. And among the cities of the children of Manasseh

* This should be "the sea" (generally used here to mean the Mediterranean Sea), not "the Salt Sea" (the Dead Sea).

were Caesarea,* Atlit, and Dora and all their towns.

29. And the lot was to the tribe of the children of Issachar to their families, on the east side, the Jordan River from the border of the tribe of the children of Manasseh to the border of the tribe of the children of Zebulun, and on the west the border of the tribe of Zebulun and the border of the tribe of Manasseh,

30. On the north side, the border of the tribe of the children of Manasseh, and on the south side, the border of the tribe of the children of Manasseh and the border of the tribe of the children of Zebulun,

31. And in this lot was the city of Genin, and the city of Gilboa, and Nuresh, and Nain.

32. And the lot was to the tribe of the children of Zebulun to their families,

33. On the east side, the Jordan River and Sea of Tiberias,† and on the west side, the Salt Sea,‡ on the north side the inheritance of the tribe of the children of Naphtali and the tribe of the children of Asher,

34. And on the south side, the inheritance of the tribe of the children of Issachar and the tribe of the children of Manasseh,

* In 22 BCE, Herod the Great expanded the ancient city named Straton's Tower and renamed it Caesaria to honor Caesar Augustus. It seems most likely that some scribe in Roman times absent-mindedly substituted the common name at his time for the ancient name in the text.

† The Sea of Galilee began to be called Lake Tiberias after the Romans built the city of Tiberias on its coast in the first century AD. In Biblical times, it was called the Sea of Chinnereth, the name that is used everywhere else in this chapter. It seems most likely that a scribe in Roman times made the error of calling it the "Sea of Tiberias."

‡ This should be "the sea" (generally used here to mean the Mediterranean Sea), not "the Salt Sea" (the Dead Sea).

35. And of the cities of its lot was Tiberias[*] and all its towns.

36. And the lot was to the tribe of the children of Asher to their families, on the ocean side the Salt Sea,[†] and on the south side, Sidon and Sor and Hamath,

37. And on the east side, the inheritance of the tribe of the children Naphtali,

38. And on the north side, the cities of Shomer, and also on the north the inheritance of the tribe of the children of Zebulun,

39. And on the east side, the inheritance of the tribe of the children of Naphtali.[‡]

40. And the lot was to the tribe of the children of Naphtali, the cities of the hill country, and on the east side,[§] the inheritance of the tribe of Asher,

41. And on the south side, the inheritance of the tribe of the children of Zebulun,

42. And among the cities of the children of Naphtali were Saphar Saphat. and Kedesh and all their towns.

43. And these are the cities of refuge, the three cities which are across the Jordan to the east,

44. The city of Bazir in the inheritance of the tribe of the children of Reuben, and the city of Gilead in the inheritance of the tribe of the children of Gad,

* Like the Sea of Tiberias, the name of the city of Tiberias is probably an error that a scribe made in Roman times.

† Again, this should be "the sea" (the Mediterranean Sea), not "the Salt Sea" (the Dead Sea).

‡ The repetition of verse 37 shows again that the text is corrupt.

§ This is another scribal error: Asher should be the western boundary of Naphtali, not the eastern boundary. Notice that verse 36 says that Naphtali is the eastern boundary of Asher.

45. And the city of Golan in the inheritance of the children of the half tribe of Manasseh,

46. And three cities in the land of Canaan, and these are their names: the city of Kedesh in the inheritance of the tribe of the children of Naphtali, the holy Shechem in the inheritance of the tribe of the children of Ephraim, the city of Hebron in the inheritance of the tribe of the children of Judah.

Chapter XV

1. And Joshua son of Nun called to all the elders of the sons of Reuben and the sons of Gad and to the half tribe of the sons of Manasseh,

2. And he said to them, You have observed all that Moses the servant of the Lord commanded you, and you have heard my voice in all that I have commanded you,

3. You have not abandoned your brothers for many days up to this day, and you have observed the charges of the Lord, your God.

4. And now the Lord your God has completed the promises to your brothers, as He spoke to them, and now turn, and go to your tents, and return to the land that Moses, the servant of the Lord, gave to you across the Jordan.

5. Only be very observant to do the commandments and the law that Moses, servant of the Lord, commanded you, to love the Lord, your God, and to go in all his ways, and to serve Him with all your heart and with all your soul.

6. And Joshua son of Nun and Eliezer son of Aaron the priest blessed them.

7. And they took Nobah, the son of Hepher, the son of Gilead, the son of Machir, the son of Manasseh, the son

of Joseph, in the sight of all the congregation of the children of Israel, and made him king over the two tribes and half tribe,

8. And they blessed him and sent him away, him and all his men, and they went to the land of their inheritance, which is across the Jordan east of Jericho, in peace.

9. And Nobah stood as judge over the two tribes and the half tribe in the city of Kenath, which he called by his name, Nobah.

Chapter XVI

1. And it happened after these things that a new king rose, and his name was Shobach, son of Hamam, son of Reuan,

2. And there were under his hand a very abundant army, and horses, and chariots, and horsemen.

3. And Shobach sent and called the remnant of the Canaanites and sent messengers to great Armina and also messengers to little Armina, and to the king of Sidon and Sor, and to the king of Damascus, and Shobach gathered the kings in Kimon, them and their armies,

4. And their hosts were a very abundant army, innumerable.

5. And Shobach wrote a letter, a royal letter, to Joshua son of Nun, from him and from the kings who were with him in Kimon,

6. And they sent the royal letter to Joshua son of Nun, to Mt. Gerizim Beth El, and this is what they wrote in it:

7. From the assembly that is gathered against you, Joshua son of Nun, and may peace be upon you,

8. We know that you are a killer wolf, and we know what you have done with our lands and with our kings,

9. And that you killed thirty-five kings,

10. And they are Sihon king of the Amorites, and Og king of Bashan,

11. And Balak the son of Zippor, and the king of Midian,

12. And the king of Jericho, and the king of Ai,

13. And the king of Jebus, the king of Hebron,

14. The king of Jarmuth, the king of Lachish,

15. The king of Eglon, the king of Gezer,

16. The king of Debir, the king of Geder.

17. The king of Hormah, the king of Arad,

18. The king of Libnah, the king of Adulam,

19. The king of Makdah, the king of Lusha,

20. The king of Tappuah, the king of Hepher,

21. The king of Afek, the king of Lascharon,

22. The king of Madon, the king of Hasor,

23. The king of Shimron, the king of Achsheaf,

24. The king of Taanach, the king of Megiddo,

25. The king of Kedesh, the king of Jokneam,

26. The king of Carmel, the king of Dor in Naphat Dor,

27. The king of Goyim in Gilgal, the king of Tirzah,

28. And you have destroyed their cities and burnt all of their places.

29. And now here we are seeking to avenge them upon you.

30. Know that we are coming to you to make war on you at the place Elon Moreh, facing Mt. Gerizim, on which you have raised your temple to serve the Lord your God,

31. And in another three days,* we will come to you and do what we speak to you.

Chapter XVII

1. And they sent this royal letter with a wise and intelligent man and commanded him to give the letter into the hand of Joshua, king of Israel.
2. And the man heard their words and went and came to Joshua son of Nun.
3. And he found him sitting on his royal throne, and he took from him an order to come to him.
4. And he gave it into the hand of Joshua, and he turned from him.
5. And he gave him an order to come to him, and he came to him on the sixth day of the seventh week.
6. And they had counted forty-eight days of the fifty days that the Lord had commanded them, His people the children of Israel, to count every year, by the hand of His servant, Moses.†
7. And Joshua took the letter from the hand of the man and read it and knew all that was in it, and he commanded to keep the man carrying the letter.
8. And the children of Israel rested on the seventh sabbath, and they celebrated the holiday of Shavuot on the next day after this seventh sabbath with joy and with goodness of heart, as the Lord had commanded by the hand of Moses His servant.

* Here the text says they will come in three days, but when Joshua replies to this letter in 19:1, he says they threatened to come within thirty days. "Three" here seems to be an error.

† The counting of the Omer begins on the day after Passover. The fiftieth day is Shavuot (Hebrew for "weeks"), called Pentecost in English. This is the forty-eighth day.

9. And Joshua son of Nun rose in the morning on the second day of the week, which was the next day after the holiday of Shavuot,

10. And he sent and gathered all the heads of the people and all their elders and officers, and he read in their ears the royal letter of Shobach and all the kings who were with him,

11. And when he had finished reading the royal letter, he said to them,

12. What do you say, oh my people, to this?

13. And they answered Joshua with one voice, All that you say to us, we will hear and we will do. We will not disobey you.

14. And Joshua wrote a return letter to king Shobach and to the kings who were with him.

15. And he read it in the ears of all the of the congregation and all the heads of the tribes of the children of Israel,

16. And this is what they wrote in it.

Chapter XVIII

1. In the name of the Lord, the greatest of the great,
2. The most merciful of the merciful,
3. Who smites evil heretics,
4. Who destroys the presumptuous and the powerful,
5. Who scatters those who are gathered,
6. Who gathers those who are scattered,
7. Who kills the living,
8. Who gives life to the dead,
9. Whose hand is strong and arm is outstretched,

10. He is above those who are high,

11. And He rules over rulers,

12. And He passes judgment on the judges,

13. Under His arm is the world,

14. And His glory in the clouds of his abode,

15. Blessed is he and blessed is his name forever.

16. After this, I am Joshua son of Nun son of Eden son of Shuthelah son of Ephraim, the son of Joseph, who reigned over all the land of Egypt,

17. A disciple of the lord of the prophets, Moses, the son of Amram, by whose hand the Lord did signs and great wonders in the land of Egypt,

18. And he brought out from there my people, the children of Israel, and he took them by way of the Red Sea, and he stretched out his hand over the sea,

19. And his people, the children of Israel, went through the sea on dry land,

20. And the water formed a wall for them on the right and left,

21. And the children of Israel came out from the sea, all of them unharmed,

22. And Pharaoh, king of Egypt, and all his army and his horses and his chariots, sank in it.

23. And now know that on me and on my people are peace and mercy, and on you, the curse and the plague. There will never be peace upon you.

Chapter XIX

1. Remember that you would come to me in another thirty days, and you said that you would come to near

Mt. Gerizim Bethel, to the place Elon Moreh, on which I serve my God and offer His sacrifices, for it is the mountain of blessings,

2. The mountain of the inheritance and of the divine presence, the place of holinesses, the shelter of higher guidance, the house of my God, the mountain of His inheritance, the place of His dwelling.

3. Do you not know that you cannot touch, cannot see, cannot stand on this place of holinesses?

4. In another three days, I will come to you,

5. And the encamped army of the congregation of Israel, which is my people, trusting in the Lord, our God, in all we do,

6. Guarding us by Himself, for He will save us from all oppression and release us from all blockades,

7. And free us from all distress, and do with us as he has done to our fathers,

8. For he knows the wickedness of your inclination and the purity of our inclination. You bow down to foreign gods who do not see, and do not hear, and do not eat, and do not smell and do not know anything,

9. But we bow down to Him only, because he is God, the God of spirits, Who knows what is hidden and what is revealed, Who answers the pure. We do not believe in other gods than Him alone.

10. And He will cleave to us in all things and will save us from all distress, and you will have no peace from Him.

Chapter XX

1. When the children of Israel heard all the words of this royal letter which Joshua son of Nun read in their ears,

2. All the people answered with one voice, and they said:
3. Praised be He who enlightens your understanding.
4. Praised be He who puts wisdom in your heart.
5. Praised be He for all your wonderful intelligence.
6. You have lifted our heads,
7. And you have strengthened our hearts,
8. And you have encouraged our strength,
9. And you have made great our memory and the memory of our children.
10. You have destroyed our enemies without a sword.
11. We hear your voice, and we will not disobey your mouth.
12. And Joshua gave the letter to the man whom Shobach sent and the men whom they sent with him,
13. And he went, panicked in his heart and his understanding, greatly awed by seeing the children of Israel and their words and their encampment and the goodness of their ways and all their hosts.
14. And he came to his congregation, grieving at heart,
15. And he gave them the royal letter of the children of Israel,
16. And he told them all the things that he had heard and that he had seen with his eyes.
17. And king Shobach called a knowledgeable man who knew the Hebrew language, and he read the royal letter in their ears and translated for them and spoke to them.
18. But he had not yet finished reading this royal letter when the people cried out loud and long, and wept and cried and rent their clothes,
19. And they said to Shobach, What is this that you have done to us? You have thrown us into a great fire.

20. Then, among the kings and their armies, Shobach saw these things and feared greatly before Joshua son of Nun and his people, the children of Israel.

21. Then he sent and called all the magicians and sorcerers present in the land of his kingdom, and also his mother, who was a witch.

22. And Shobach said to them, What do you think about this thing for which we have abandoned our lives, and we did not remember the deeds of our enemies since they came out of the land of Egypt until this day and all the miracles and signs and wonders that they have done?

23. And the magicians answered Shobach and the kings who were with him, Stand fast and do not fear, and see the deeds that we will do to Joshua son of Nun and to all the children of Israel, his people.

24. And the mother of Shobach said to her son, My son, do not fear and do not tremble before the children of Israel and Joshua son of Nun,

25. And see what your mother will do to them, for tomorrow, they will all perish before you. Do not fear, and do not tremble.

Chapter XXI

1. And Joshua son of Nun chose from all the children of Israel twenty thousand men of war,

2. And Phinehas son of Eliezer the priest for the army, the holy vessels. and the blast trumpets in his hand,

3. And they went to war against Shobach and against the kings gathered with him, and they went, and they came to Elon Kimon,

4. And at the time they arrived at that place, the magi-

cians did their works on them, and Joshua and all the men who were with him were trapped in that place,

5. And these children of Israel were trapped in Elon Kimon, and they did not know what to do, and they were not able to get out and to go.

6. Then Joshua stood and prayed to the Lord, God of Israel to deliver him from this trouble, him and all the people who were with him,

7. And he said, Lord, my lord, turn from the wrath of Your anger and repent of the evil upon Your people,

8. Lord, my lord, you have shown your servant Your greatness and Your strong hand; what God is there in heaven or on earth who can do such deeds and such power?

9. Turn from the wrath of Your anger and repent of the evil upon Your people.

10. Remember Abraham, Isaac, and Jacob, Your servants, to whom you swore by Yourself,

11. And the righteous acts of my father Joseph, whom You loved, and Moses son of Amram, faithful to Your house,

12. See that now we are trapped. With Your salvation, save us from the hand of our enemies, and send an angel* to us to keep us.

13. And Joshua fell down, and behold a dove stood before him, and it went and stood between his hands,

14. And Joshua hurried and wrote a royal letter to Nobach, son of his uncle, and said to him,

15. My son, at the time you read this letter, you will have awakened from your sleep. And when you have awak-

* The Hebrew word for angel also means "messenger," so Joshua's prayer is answered when the dove appears and acts as his messenger..

ened, stand on your feet. And when you have stood, come to us. And when you have come, hurry to us.

16. And know that I and all your brothers, the children of Israel who are with me, are trapped in the midst of seven iron walls in Elon Kimon.

17. And Joshua put the letter in the beak of the dove, and it took it in its beak and flew.

18. And in a moment, it reached the city of Kenath, and it cast the royal letter in the lap of Nobach,

19. And he saw the letter, and he opened it, and he read all the words that were in it,

20. And he raised his voice, and he wept, and he put sackcloth on his loins, and he cried out a great and very bitter cry.

21. And he said, Speedily, speedily, children of my people.

22. And all the men of his city heard, and all the men of the two and a half tribes heard,

23. And all the men of war gathered to him, and there was a great cry, as there had never been the like in Israel

24. And Nobach said to them, Hurry, my brothers, hurry. Do not stand still. For my uncle's son, Joshua and the army that is with him are all trapped in the midst of seven iron walls in Elon Kimon.

25. So the men of the army heard this word from Nobach, and they hurried, and they went, and they came to the land of Canaan, to Elon Kimon, soon.

26. And they made a great war with king Shobach and with the kings who were with him.

27. And Nobach dominated Shobach and all who were with him and smote them with the edge of the sword.

28. And Nobach called, and he said to Phinehas son of Eliezer the priest, Blow the blast trumpets that are in your hand.
29. And they blew on them, and the steel walls that surrounded them dissolved, and Joshua and the men who were with him came out in peace. Not a man of them was missing.
30. And on that day, the Lord gave Shobach and all who were with him into the hand of Israel.

Chapter XXII

1. And it happened at the end of many days after the Lord had given Israel rest from all their enemies around them,
2. And Joshua son of Nun was old and full of days,
3. And Joshua gathered all the tribes of the children of Israel to Shechem,
4. And he called all the elders of the children of Israel, and their heads, and their judges, and their chiefs,
5. And they went up to the chosen place, Mt. Gerizim Bethel, and they came together before God at the opening of the tent of meeting.
6. And Joshua son of Nun said to them, I am dying, and I am going from among you.*
7. And you know all that the Lord has done for you.
8. And He took your fathers out from the land of Egypt with signs, and with wonders, and with war, and with a strong hand, and with an outstretched arm, and with

* In the equivalent passage in Jos 23:14, Joshua says before dying "I am going today on the way of all things of earth," similar to what King David says before dying.

great power, and you crossed the Red Sea on dry land.

9. And He gave you the land you had not labored in and cities you had not built, and you dwelt in them. You eat vineyards and olive trees you did not plant.

10. And now, fear the Lord, your God, and serve Him with all your strength, with simplicity, and with faith, and do not serve any but the Lord, your God, Himself.

11. And if it is bad in your eyes to serve the Lord, your God, choose for yourselves today whom you will serve, if it is the Lord, your God, or if it is the gods of the nations in whose land you dwell. But I and my house, we will not serve any except the Lord, our God, Himself.

12. And all the people answered and said, Far be it from us to leave the Lord, our God, to serve other gods.

13. For we will serve the Lord, our God, for He is our God and the God of our fathers.

14. And Joshua said to the people, You are witnesses to yourselves, for you have chosen the Lord for yourselves, to serve Him.

15. And they said, We are witnesses.

16. And Joshua son of Nun made a covenant with the people on that day, and he gave to them an ordinance and a judgment in the holy city of Shechem, which is at the foot of Mt. Gerizim Bethel, and he made it the seat of judgment.

17. And he wrote these words in a book, and he gave it to the priests, the sons of Levi, and he said to them, Take this book and watch over it.

18. And they took a great stone and set it up there under the oak that was at the foot of Mt. Gerizim, the place of the sanctuary of the Lord.

19. And Joshua said to the people, Behold this stone will be a witness for us,

20. And he built an altar there under the mountain, and he took one ram from the sheep, and he sacrificed it on account of this covenant which the children of Israel made with him.

21. And after this, Joshua son of Nun chose twelve leaders from the leaders of the children of Israel, one man for each tribe,

22. And he cast lots among them according to the word of Eliezer son of Aaron, the priest in the chosen place, Mt. Gerizim Bethel, before the Lord. And the lot for kingship over the children of Israel fell to a man named Nathaniel, son of the brother of Caleb, from the tribe of Judah, and he made him king over the children of Israel.

23. And it happened after these things that Joshua son of Nun, servant of the Lord, died at the age of one hundred ten years,

24. And they buried him in a hill that faced the chosen place, Mt. Gerizim Bethel, in Mattenath Zerah, and the children of Israel wept for him for thirty days, and the days of weeping for him were complete.

Chapter XXIII

1. And Nathaniel son of Kenaz and the son of the brother of Caleb from the tribe of the children of Judah was king over the children of Israel.

2. And it happened in the fourth year of the reign of Nathaniel son of Kenaz that Eliezer son of Aaron the priest died, and all the days of his priesthood were fifty years in the chosen place, Mt. Gerizim Bethel.

3. And it happened that his day to die was close, and he called all the Levite priests and all the elders of Israel to the holy city of Shechem, and the heads of the people gathered together in Shechem,

4. And they went up according to the word of Eliezer the priest to the chosen place, Mt. Gerizim Bethel,

5. And he said to them, Watch over yourselves, lest you be deceived and turn aside from the way that Moses, servant of the Lord, commanded you according to the word of the Lord.

6. Observe all the words of this law, for it is your wisdom and your understanding in the eyes of all the peoples,

7. And do not turn aside from the truth to the right or to the left.

8. And Eliezer took one ram and sacrificed it as a sacrifice upon this covenant on the altar of the Lord.

9. And he bowed down before the altar and before the ark of the testimony, and he removed his clothes and put them on Phinehas, his son.

10. And he went out from there, and he went on his feet, the Levite priests and all the leaders of the children of Israel on his right and on his left, until they reached the town of Amartah,

11. And all the Levite priests and all the elders of the people and their officers and heads stood before him,

12. And Phinehas, his son, his successor, was standing to his right, and tears flowed from his eyes on account of the end of his father,

13. And all the house of the priests did as he did.

14. And they all went until they reached the hill of Phinehas, his son, and there he renewed the covenant with them, saying,

15. Watch over yourselves lest you serve other gods, lest your burnt offerings go up on every place you see, but only in this place, Mt. Gerizim Bethel, where the Lord, your God, chose for his name to dwell.
16. And Eliezer expired, and died, and was gathered to his people. And they buried him in the hill of Phinehas, his son, at the foot of the holy mountain, the place that the Lord chose, Mt. Gerizim.
17. It was he who wrote the true calculation tested for the width of Mt. Gerizim Bethel, and he calculated the beginning of the months from the phases of the moon and the sun, that from it you know the days of the appointed times and the months and the years.*

Chapter XXIV

1. And Phinehas son of Eliezer son of Aaron the priest begot a son in the year that the children of Israel arrived in Canaan, and he called his name Abishah.
2. And Abishah, the male heir, in the thirteenth year after the children of Israel crossed into Canaan, which was the thirteenth year of the days of his life, wrote the holy book of the Torah† which is found in the holy city of Shechem in the house of the priests to this day.
3. And this writing was written on Mt. Gerizim Bethel at the opening of the tent of meeting, and it is found in it without any addition or subtraction.

* This verse apparently means that he created a calendar to keep track of the new moons, the appointed times for holidays, and the beginning of the new year. The dates are based on the lunar calendar, and the days begin when the sun sets at Mt. Gerizim.

† Before this point, we have translated the Hebrew Torah as "Law," but here it clearly refers to the scroll that the Samaritans have in Shechem with their version of the entire Torah.

4. And the skins are from the skins of peace offerings that the congregation sacrificed on the altar.

5. And its provenance is in letters among the columns of of the words of the Torah in letters recognizable among the columns,

6. And its provenance begins with "And it will happen that when He brings you,"* which is shortly after "Hear O Israel,"†

7. And this is the complete provenance:

8. I, Abishah, son of Phinehas, son of Eleazar, son of Aaron the priest, to them be the favor of the Lord and His glory, wrote this holy book at the opening of the tent of meeting on Mt. Gerizim Bethel in the thirteenth year of the dwelling of the children of Israel in the land of Canaan. I thank the Lord.

The Lord return on us His blessing, and the blessing of the one who wrote it with his holy hand, and the blessing of the dwelling of the name of the Lord at whose opening it was written, and the blessing of the chosen place where it was written according to the work of Moses the faithful one. Amen.

[Colophon of Codex B]

This book, which is called the Book of Joshua, the servant of our lord Moses, peace be upon him, was finished in Ramesh‡ on the fifth day,§ the thirty-fourth of the fifty

* Deut 11:29

† Deut 6:4. The Torah scroll does not have chapters and verses, so they use this well known passage to help locate the the passage that is the beginning of the acrostic.

‡ Possibly Rameh, a town in what is now the northern part of Israel.

§ Thursday

days that the Lord commanded us to count,* and that is 20 of the second month, as it is called in the Arabic language, of year one thousand three hundred and twenty-two,† and ten of the reign of the sons of Haggar, by the hand of the wretched, poor, needy servant Abishah son of Phinehas son of Isaac, the Levite priest, sexton of the holy places. May the Lord forgive him all sin, transgression and crime, and keep his soul apart from sins through the merit of the three worthy ones and Joseph and Moses, the man of God.

Amen, Amen, Amen.
Mercy, Mercy, Mercy.
Oh, Answerer of questions.

[Colophon of Codex C]

The writing of this holy book was completed on the fourth day,‡ 19 of the month one,§ of the year three thousand five hundred and forty seven of the dwelling of the children of Israel in the land of Canaan by the hand of the unfortunate Jacob son of Aaron the priest, may the Lord send him faith through the merit of Moses the faithful one. Amen.

* Jews and Samaritans count fifty days from the day after Passover until Sukkot.

† 1322 on the Muslim calendar is 1904.

‡ Wednesday

§ Nineteenth of Nisan.

About the Arabic Text of the Samaritan Book of Joshua

The Arabic version of the Samaritan Book of Joshua clearly was written later than the Hebrew version, at a time when the Samaritans were so strongly influenced by Muslim culture it does not seem to be in the style of a Biblical text, as the earlier Hebrew version is. The translation by Oliver Turnbull Crane, published in 1890, makes it seem even more remote by keeping the Arabic versions of the Hebrew names rather than translating them to English, though it provides the English version in parentheses the first time it is used: for example, throughout the text, it uses Musa rather than Moses and Yush'a rather than Joshua, and it even uses "imam" instead of "high priest."

In addition to covering the same material as the Hebrew text of the Samaritan book of Joshua, it has a long additions at the beginning (Chapters 1 to 8), which covers events that happened in the desert before Moses died, and an even longer addition at the end (Chapters 39-50), which covers the history of Israel to Roman times; though the ending is lost, Crane includes a note saying that the Samaritans told him that it continued to the time of the coming of the messiah.

The addition at the beginning is interesting largely because it includes a rational attempt to make sense of the story of Balaam in the Torah. The Torah talks about Balaam in two places. One version (Num 22-24), edited together from the E text and the J text, depicts Balaam as a sympathetic character: he is hired to curse the Israelites, but he learns from a dream (E text) or from his donkey, which suddenly speaks (J text) that the Lord is protecting the Israelites, and so he becomes sympathetic to them. There is a briefer mention of him in the P text (Num 31:8-16), which depicts Balaam as hostile to the Israelites, misleading them in the matter of Peor and being killed by the Israelites. The story here tries to reconcile the two, as Balaam explains that he was always hostile to the Israelites but did not act on his hostility earlier by cursing them because he did not dare to disobey the Lord. The P text of the Torah, written by Jerusalem priests, condemns him; it is interesting that, in this much later text, the Samaritan priests who were descended from the Jerusalem priests, still condemn him. The Torah was canonized and could not be altered, so this story of Balaam was added to the Samaritan Book of Joshua, where it is out of place.

The addition at the end is interesting because it extends the story beyond the death of Joshua, describing the golden age when Joshua's successors ruled as kings of Israel and sacrificed at Mt. Gerizim and the decline that happened when the Ark moved to Shiloh at the time when Eli was high priest at Shiloh, a time described at the beginning of the book of I Samuel, and the history beyond that (with many gaps) culminating in the predicted coming of a messiah who will reestablish the Temple on Mt. Gerizim, presumably beginning a new golden age. It drops the story of how the Torah was written down which is at the end of the Hebrew text (SJos 24) and is the climax of that book, in favor of this Messianic climax.

Throughout, it also keep the Jerusalem priests' habit of dating events, which we see in the P text. For example, Chapter 46, which describes the time of Alexander the Great, begins, "The whole number of the years from Adam up to the time of king el-Iskandar was three thousand nine hundred and thirty years."

It makes sense to call the Hebrew version The Book of Joshua, but so much additional history was added to the Arabic version that more than half of it is not about Joshua at all, so Crane titled it *The Samaritan Chronicle or the Book of Joshua the Son of Nun*.

Notes

1.See Benyamim Tsedaka, translator and editor, Sharon Sullivan, editor, James Charlesworth, introduction, *The Israelite Samaritan Version of the Torah: First English Translation Compared with the Masoretic Version* (Eerdmans, 2013).

2. Peter J. Oefner, Peidong Shen, George Höltz, Isaac Shpirer, Dov Gefel, Tal Lavi, Eilon Wool, Jonathan Cohen, Cengiz Cinnioglu, Peter A. Underhill, Noah A. Rosenberg, Jochen Hochrein, Julie M. Granka, Hossi Hillel, Marcus W. Feldman, "Genetics and the History of the Samaritans: Y-Chromosomal Microsatellites and Genetic Affinity between Samaritans and Cohanim". *Human Biology 85*, 2013, pp. 825–858.

See also Diana Muir Appelbaum, Paul Appelbaum, "Genetics and the Jewish identity, *The Jerusalem Post*, November 2, 2008.

3. James A. Montgomery, *The Samaritans, The Earliest Jewish Sect; Their History, Theology and Literature* (J.C. Winston Co, 1907) p. 56.

4. Josephus, *Antiquities of the Jews*, Chapter 8: Concerning Sanballat And Manasseh, And The Temple Which They Built On Mount Gerizzim; As Also How Alexander Made His Entry Into The City Jerusalem, And What Benefits He Bestowed On The Jews.

5. Josephus, *Antiquities of the Jews*, 9:1.

6. Magnar Kartveit, "The Second Temple and the Temple of the Samaritans," in Jörg Frey, Ursula Schattner-Rieser, Kon-

rad Schmid, eds, *The Samaritans and the Bible* (De Gruyter, 2012) pp. 70-71.

7. Yitzhak Magen, "The Dating of the First Phase of the Samaritan Temple on Mount Gerizim in Light of the Archaeological Evidence," in Oded Lipschits, Gary N. Knoppers, Rainer Albertz, eds., *Judah and the Judeans in the Fourth Century B.C.E.* (Penn State University Press, 2007) pp. 158.

8. James Hamilton Charlesworth, "The Discovery of an Unknown Dead Sea Scroll: The Original Text of Deuteronomy 27?" *OWU: The Magazine of Ohio Wesleyan University*, Summer 2012.

9. Josephus, *Antiquities of the Jews*, 9:1.

10. Montgomery, *The Samaritans*, pp. 151-152.

11. *The Samaritan Update: An Internet Newsletter & Archive Regarding the Samaritan-Israelites*, "The Samaritans call themselves Bene-Yisrael 'Children of Israel', or Shamerim 'Observant Ones,' March 4, 2024.

12. See Charles Siegel, *The P Text Untangled: Making Sense of the Most Puzzling Text of the Bible* (Omo Press, 2025) pp. 15-18.

13. See Charles Siegel, *The Bible Untangled: Read the Texts that Were Edited Together Thousands of Years Ago to Form the Early Books of the Bible* (Omo Press, 2019).

14. Israel Finkelstein and Neil Asher Silberman, *The Bible Unearthed: Archeology's New Vision of Ancient Israel and the Origin of Its Sacred Texts* (Simon and Schuster, 2001) p. 114.

15. Finkelstein and Silberman, *The Bible Unearthed*, p. 114.

16. The earliest reference to Israel that archeologists have found is the Merneptah Stele, erected by the Egyptians as a victory monument in 1208 BCE. Kenton L Sparks, *Ethnicity and Identity in Ancient Israel* (Eisenbrauns, 1998) pp. 96-97.

17. William G. Dever, *Who Were the Early Israelites and Where Did They Come From* (Eerdmans, 2003) p. 45.

18. Finkelstein, *The Bible Unearthed*, p. 109, Dever, *Who Were the Early Israelites?*, p. 126.

19. Finkelstein, *The Bible Unearthed*, p. 107, Dever, *Who Were the Early Israelites?* p. 118.

20. Finkelstein, *The Bible Unearthed*, p. 143.

21. Avraham Biran, Joseph Naveh, "The Tel Dan Inscription: A New Fragment," *Israel Exploration Journal*, 45:1, 1995, pp. 1–18.

22. Archeological surveys have shown that there was a destruction of Philistine cities at the time of David, but pottery, architecture, and other elements of material culture remained the same after this destruction. If the Israelites had driven out the Philistines and taken this land for themselves, the Philistine material culture would have been replaced by Israelite material culture. The Philistine styles continued after the destruction, showing that David probably attacked the cities and then made them pay tribute to avoid further attacks, rather than taking over their territory as part of an Israelite empire. Finkelstein, *The Bible Unearthed*, pp. 131-135.

www.ingramcontent.com/pod-product-compliance
Lightning Source LLC
LaVergne TN
LVHW010106110826
845155LV00028B/501

* 9 7 8 1 9 4 1 6 6 7 6 0 6 *